The
Specter
of
Munich

Also by Jeffrey Record

Dark Victory: America's Second War Against Iraq

Making War, Thinking History: Munich, Vietnam, and Presidential Uses of Force from Korea to Kosovo

The Wrong War: Why We Lost in Vietnam

Hollow Victory: A Contrary View of the Gulf War

Beyond Military Reform: American Defense Dilemmas

Revising U.S. Military Strategy: Tailoring Means to Ends

The
Specter
of
Munich

Reconsidering the Lessons
of Appeasing Hitler

Jeffrey Record

Potomac Books, Inc.
Washington, D.C.

Library of Congress Cataloging-in-Publication Data

Record, Jeffrey.
  The specter of Munich : reconsidering the lessons of appeasing Hitler
/ Jeffrey Record. — 1st ed.
      p. cm.
  Includes bibliographical references and index.
  ISBN 978-1-59797-039-6 (alk. paper)
  1. World War, 1939-1945—Diplomatic history. 2. World War, 1939-
1945—Causes. 3. Munich Four-Power Agreement (1938) I. Title.
  D748.R44 2006
  940.53'112—dc22

                              2006008922

ISBN 978-1-59797-040-2 (paperback)

The views expressed in this book are the author's own and do not
necessarily represent those of the Air War College, Air Force,
Department of Defense, or any other federal government agency.

Potomac Books, Inc.
22841 Quicksilver Drive
Dulles, Virginia 20166

First Edition
10 9 8 7 6 5 4 3 2 1

There was never a war in all history easier to prevent by timely action than the one which has just desolated great areas of the globe. It could have been prevented without the firing of a single shot, but no one would listen.

—Winston Churchill, 1946[1]

Appeasement in itself may be good or bad according to the circumstances. Appeasement from weakness and fear is alike futile and fatal. Appeasement from strength is magnanimous and noble, and might be the surest and only path to world peace.

—Winston Churchill, 1950[2]

CONTENTS

Chronology   ix
Map: Europe after World War I   18
Map: Nazi Germany's Expansion, 1936–39   19

1. Introduction:
    The Staying Power of the Munich Analogy   1

2. Why Britain and France Appeased Hitler   13

3. Why Appeasement Failed   67

4. Appeasement's Lessons for the United States
    Today   73

5. Concluding Observations and
    Recommendations   111

Notes   130
Bibliography   146
Index   156
About the Author   164

Toward the Second World War: A Chronology of Events

1919

June: Treaty of Versailles is imposed on Germany.

1931

September: Japan occupies Manchuria.

1932

November: Franklin D. Roosevelt is elected President of the United States.

1933

January: Adolph Hitler is appointed German Chancellor.

February: Japan leaves the League of Nations.

October: Germany leaves the League of Nations.

1935

March: Hitler announces repudiation of the arms limitation clauses of the Treaty of Versailles and the reintroduction of conscription.

June: Anglo-German Naval Agreement permits Germany to build a navy one-third the strength of the Royal Navy.

1936

March: German troops reoccupy the Rhineland.

October: Germany and Italy conclude a defensive alliance.

November: Germany and Japan conclude an anti-Soviet alliance.

1937

May: Neville Chamberlain becomes British prime minister and pledges to support a policy of appeasement toward Germany and Italy.

July: Japan invades China.

1938

March: Germany occupies and incorporates Austria.

September: In the Munich Agreement, Britain, France, Germany, and Italy agree to transfer Czechoslovakia's Sudetenland to Germany.

October: Chamberlain proclaims the Munich Agreement to be "peace in our time."

1939

March: Germany invades the rest of Czechoslovakia; Britain and France offer a defense guarantee to Poland against a German attack.

August: Hitler and Stalin conclude a non-aggression pact.

September: Germany invades Poland; Britain and France declare war on Germany.

1940

May: Winston Churchill replaces Chamberlain as British prime minister.

May–June: Germany invades and defeats France and the Low Countries.

August–September: The Royal Air Force defeats the Luftwaffe's attempt to gain air superiority over the British Isles.

1941

June: Hitler invades the Soviet Union.

December: The Japanese attack Pearl Harbor; the United States declares war on Japan; Germany declares war on the United States; the United States declares war on Germany.

1

Introduction:
The Staying Power of
the Munich Analogy

NO HISTORICAL EVENT has exerted more influence on post–World War II U.S. presidential use-of-force decisions than the Anglo–French appeasement of Nazi Germany that led to the outbreak of World War II. The great lesson drawn from appeasement—namely, that capitulating to the demands of territorially aggressive dictatorships simply makes inevitable a later, larger war on less favorable terms—has informed most major U.S. uses of force since the surrender of Nazi Germany and Imperial Japan in 1945.[1] From the Truman administration's 1950 decision to fight in Korea to the George W. Bush administration's 2003 decision to invade Iraq, presidents repeatedly have relied on the Munich analogy to determine what to do in a perceived security crisis. They have also employed that analogy as a tool for mobilizing public opinion for military action.[2]

It was of course at the Munich conference of September–October 1938 that Britain and France bowed to Hitler's threat of war and ceded the German-speaking areas of Czechoslovakia to Nazi Germany. In so doing, Britain and France not only sacrificed eastern Europe's only democracy to Adolf Hitler but also earned the utter contempt of the German dictator. Hitler subsequently invaded the rest of Czechoslovakia.

As the United States approached its second war with Iraq, neoconservatives and other war proponents cited the consequences of the democracies' appeasement of the burgeoning Nazi menace during the 1930s and asserted that war was necessary to remove Saddam Hussein before he acquired the nuclear weapons with which he would threaten and even attack the United States. Munich's great lesson, they argued, was to move early and decisively against rising security threats. World War II could have been avoided had the democracies been prepared to stop Hitler's remilitarization of the Rhineland in 1936 or to fight for Czechoslovakia in 1938. Instead, they did nothing when a mere three German army battalions crossed over to the Rhine's left bank, and they handed over vital chunks of Czech territory. With each act of appeasement Hitler's appetite grew. Thus military action against a prenuclear Saddam Hussein in 2003 would be much easier and less risky than war with a nuclear Saddam later on. War with Saddam, as with Hitler, was in any event inevitable, so it was better to have it now on more favorable terms rather than later on less favorable ones.

Neoconservative Richard Perle, the influential chairman of the Defense Policy Board, argued in an August 2002 interview with the *London Daily Telegraph*,

> [An] action to remove Saddam could precipitate the very thing we are most anxious to prevent: his use of chemical and biological weapons. But the danger that springs from his capabilities will only grow as he expands his arsenal. A preemptive strike against Hitler at the time of Munich would have meant an immediate war, as opposed to the one that came later. Later was much worse.[3]

In that same month Secretary of Defense Donald Rumsfeld, in a television interview in which arose the issue of evidence of Saddam Hussein's weapons of mass destruction, opined, "Think of all the countries that said, 'Well, we don't have enough evidence.' *Mein Kampf* had been written. Hitler had indicated what he intended to do. Maybe he won't attack us. . . . Well, there are millions of dead because of those miscalculations." Later he added, "Maybe Winston Churchill was right. Maybe that lone voice expressing concerns about what was happening was right." As early as January 2002 President George W. Bush was speaking about using preventive war as a means of dealing with a rising enemy bent on domination. "Time is not on our side," he said in his State of the Union address. "I will not wait on events while dangers gather. I will not stand by as peril draws closer and closer. The United States will not permit the world's most dangerous regimes to threaten us with the world's most dangerous weapons."[4]

For neoconservatives, who have provided the intellectual foundation of U.S. foreign policy since the September 11, 2001, terrorist attacks (enshrined in President Bush's September 2002 *The National Security Strategy of the United States of America*),[5] the failure of the democracies to stop Hitler in the 1930s remains the primary instruction on both international politics and America's role in the world. Andrew Bacevich, in his trenchant assessment of the propositions that comprise the essence of neoconservative thinking on foreign policy, identifies "the first and most fundamental proposition" to be "a theory of history" based on "two large truths" originating from the decade of the 1930s—namely, that "evil is real" and that "for evil to prevail requires only one thing: for those confronted by it to flinch from duty."[6] From this proposition flows (1) the imperative of possessing irresistible military power and a willingness to use it, (2) the identification of the United States as the only power capable of standing up to evil, and (3) the necessary dedication of the United States to the mission of removing evil from the world. As President Bush declared just three days after the 9/11 attacks, "our responsibility to history is already clear: to answer these attacks and rid the world of evil."[7]

Presidential invocation of the Munich analogy as an argument for the use of force began during the run-up to the Korean War. For Harry Truman, the analogy dictated U.S. intervention: "Communism was acting in Korea just as Hitler and the Japanese had acted ten, fifteen, twenty years earlier."[8] A year after the Korean War ended, Dwight Eisenhower, citing the "domino effects" of a Communist victory in Indochina on the rest of Southeast Asia, invoked Munich in an appeal for Anglo–American military action: "We failed to halt Hirohito, Mussolini, and Hitler by not acting in unity and in time. . . . May it not be that [we] have learned something from that lesson?"[9] Indeed, Eisenhower was the first to publicly propound the domino theory, which holds that aggression unchecked is aggression encouraged. John F. Kennedy cited the Munich analogy during the Cuban Missile Crisis, warning that the "1930s taught us a clear lesson: aggressive conduct, if allowed to go unchecked, ultimately leads to war."[10]

The analogy also indisputably propelled the United States into the Vietnam War. Years after the war Lyndon Johnson told historian Doris Kearns, "Everything I knew about history told me that if I got out of Vietnam and let Ho Chi Minh run through the streets of Saigon, then I'd be doing exactly what Chamberlain did. . . . I'd be giving a fat reward to aggression."[11] Richard Nixon also believed Munich applied to Vietnam. In his memoirs, he approvingly quoted Churchill's condemnation of the 1938 Munich agreement and then went on to conclude that "what had been true of the betrayal of Czechoslovakia to Hitler in 1938 was no less true of the betrayal of South Vietnam to the communists advocated by many in 1965."[12]

Ronald Reagan saw in the Soviet Union a replay of the challenges the democracies faced in the 1930s and invoked the Munich analogy to justify a major U.S. military buildup as well as U.S. intervention in Grenada and Nicaragua. "One of the great tragedies of this century," he remarked in a 1983 speech, "was that it was only after the balance of power was allowed to erode and a ruthless adversary, Adolf Hitler, deliberately weighed the risks and decided to strike that the importance of a strong defense was realized."[13] Shortly after Saddam Hussein's invasion of Kuwait, President George H. W. Bush, the last occupant of the White House to perform military service in World War II, declared, "If history teaches anything, it is that we must resist aggression or it will destroy our freedoms. Appeasement does not work. As was the case in the 1930s, we see in Saddam Hussein an aggressive dictator threatening his neighbors."[14]

The influence of the Munich analogy has persisted beyond the generation of decision makers who served in World War II. President Bill Clinton, the first president born after World War II, did not hesitate to invoke the Munich analogy against Serbian dictator Slobodan Milošević. "What if someone had listened to Winston Churchill and stood up to Adolf Hitler earlier?" Clinton asked shortly before going to war over Kosovo. "How many people's lives might have been saved? And how many American lives might have been saved?"[15] George W. Bush, like his father before him, painted Saddam Hussein as an Arab Hitler bent on acquiring unstoppable power (nuclear weapons) and pursuing an agenda of aggression (domination of the Persian Gulf). On the eve of launching Operation Iraqi Freedom he observed that in "the twentieth century, some chose to appease murderous dictators, whose threats were allowed to grow into genocide and global war."[16]

Though presidents can and have, knowingly and unwittingly, misused the Munich analogy to describe security threats and the consequences of failing to act against them, there is no gainsaying the power of that analogy to mobilize public opinion.[17] This is so because of the catastrophic failure of the security policies Britain and France pursued vis-à-vis Germany in the 1930s. In retrospect, Anglo–French appeasement, driven by perceived military weakness and fear of war, did nothing but whet Hitler's insatiable territorial appetite (and his contempt for British and French political leadership) while simultaneously undermining the democracies' security. The results were the most destructive war in history and an enduring pejorative image of appeasement, which casts Nazi ideology as a self-evident blueprint of Germany's territorial aims, Neville Chamberlain as a coward and fool bent on peace at any price, Britain and France as betrayers of brave little Czechoslovakia, and Hitler as the great winner at the Munich conference of September 1938.

This is the image of appeasement that presidents have employed to justify military action over inaction in response to perceived security threats. The great strategic lesson of the 1930s, however, was drawn against a rising security threat that arguably has had no analog since the destruction of Nazi Germany and Imperial Japan. Security threats truly Hitlerian in scope are rare. Since 1945 what aggressor state has possessed the combination of vast territorial ambitions, military power, and willingness to gamble strategically that Nazi Germany possessed in 1939? Certainly not North Vietnam or Saddam Hussein's Iraq, both targets of U.S. presidential invocation of the Munich analogy. To be sure, the Soviet Union had great military power and imperial ambitions, but Stalin and his successors (Khrushchev in 1961–62 excepted) were far more patient and cautious men than Hitler, and Soviet use of force was in any event checked, to a degree that Hitler never was in peacetime, by America's nuclear deterrent and the North Atlantic Treaty Organization's containment of Communism on the ground in Europe. China may turn out to be America's next great strategic rival, but the extent of her imperial ambitions in East Asia (beyond Taiwan) remains unclear. China is moreover greatly dependent on access to the American market for her economic progress and is increasingly dependent on oil from a Persian Gulf where U.S. military hegemony remains unchallenged.

This is not to argue that threats need be as serious as Nazi Germany's to justify military action. Saddam Hussein's aggression against Kuwait in 1990 was unacceptable because it violated a cardinal international political norm and because it challenged U.S. domination in a region of vital interest to the West. Similarly, Serbian aggression in the former Yugoslavia had to be stopped because it was genocidal and threatened NATO's integrity. The Taliban also had to be driven from power because they provided a sanctuary for the 9/11 attackers.

The problem with the invocation of Munich is its suggestion that aggressor states are inherently insatiable and that failure to act against them automatically endangers U.S. security. In fact, most aggressor states have limited territorial objectives, and in some cases satisfaction of those objectives may be of little consequence to U.S.

security. North Vietnam's objectives were confined to the former French Indochina, a place of little intrinsic strategic value to the United States. Yet the Johnson administration painted Ho Chi Minh as the spear point of a concerted Sino–Soviet imperialism and claimed that a Communist victory in South Vietnam would topple dominoes all over Southeast Asia. Saddam Hussein was certainly Hitlerian in his brutality, recklessness, and appetite for aggression, but the military threat he posed was never a match for the power the United States could—and did in 1990–91—mobilize against him. By 2003 the Iraqi threat had been broken by twelve years of war and sanctions, though Saddam continued to run a monstrous tyranny and to defy United Nations (UN) demands that he account for suspected prohibited weapons stocks. Europe of the 1930s had no counterpart to the U.S. superpowerdom in the Gulf over the past two decades. Stephen Rock observes that "not every state that makes demands has unlimited ambitions."[18] Unfortunately, notes Robert Jervis, "Our memories of Hitler have tended to obscure the fact that most states are unwilling to pay an exorbitant price for a chance at expansion."[19]

If it is important to understand the rarity of genuinely Hitlerian threats, it is no less important to recognize that France and Britain faced security challenges and dilemmas in the 1930s that were too daunting and complex to be distilled into the simple choice between the "good" of stopping Hitler militarily and the "evil" of appeasing him politically. Though allies in the Great War, France and Britain still did not fully trust one another (much of Britain's social elite was Germanophile, and much of its political elite was Gallophobic[20]). Until the late 1930s, moreover, London and Paris differed profoundly on how to deal with Hitler, a function in part of differing vulnerabilities to German land power and in part of differing views on the wisdom of the 1919 Treaty of Versailles. Though Britain was more geographically secure, it faced not only a perceived direct German air threat but also increasingly threatened imperial interests in the Mediterranean and East Asia. The defense of the British Isles competed with the defense of the British Empire. Additionally, with respect to Nazi Germany, Britain also had to wrestle with the question of whether it could limit its liability in a future European war to the provision of naval power and airpower (banking on sufficient continental allies to supply the ground forces).

For its part, France, plagued by governmental instability (between 1932 and 1940 there were no fewer than sixteen coalition governments in Paris[21]) and acute internal political divisions that culminated in the defeatism and collaboration of 1940, sought to "contain" Germany through a system of alliances that would confront Berlin with the prospect of a two-front war. From 1936 on, however, France never displayed the will and military capacity necessary to convince potential eastern allies (or even Belgium, for that matter) that in the event of war it was prepared to defend them by attacking Germany. Additionally, France believed it could not act without Britain, but Britain would not act at all until Hitler had isolated London and Paris from the rest of Europe. Given these circumstances, together with a gross overestimation of the German strategic air threat, it is hardly surprising that senior British and French military leaders throughout the period 1933–39 unanimously counseled against risking war with Germany. Going to war against professional military advice is a very risky business for any democratic politician unless he has the electorate behind him, which British Prime Minister Neville Chamberlain did not in 1938 but finally did in 1939.

Harry Hearder, in his foreword to the second edition of P. M. H. Bell's *The Origins of the Second World War in Europe*, perhaps the most objective assessment of the causes of World War II published to date, concludes that "a blanket condemnation" of appeasement "is too imprecise to be tenable, and, indeed, explains nothing." He further deplores the continuing influence of the appeasement myth:

> The trouble is that vague, sweeping generalizations tend to be accepted by an ill-informed public, and build themselves up into powerful myths. Such generalizations may be accepted by the media and the public for several decades after they have been

discarded by most professional historians. Most journalists seem to think that the policy of appeasement was, in each of the relevant crises, cowardly and mistaken. They do not distinguish between the factors that were operative in 1936 from those operative in 1938, or, again, in 1939.[22]

Indeed, appeasement was never about peace at any price; had it been, neither Britain nor France would have gone to war in September 1939 over a Poland neither was in a position to defend. Appeasement was about war avoidance consistent with preservation of vital national interests, and prominent among such interests for Britain was the historic imperative of preventing Europe's domination by a hostile power. For centuries, it had been established British policy to oppose the rise of any continental hegemon. A Europe controlled by a single power was regarded as a threat to Britain's very survival. Thus Britain waged war against Philip II's Spain, Napoleonic France, Imperial Germany—and Nazi Germany.

■ ■ ■ ■

This book explores why Britain and France chose to appease Nazi Germany, assesses the causes of appeasement's failure, and identifies and explores strategic lessons of the 1930s relevant to the challenges U.S. foreign and military policies confront today. Those lessons include the importance of (1) correctly gauging enemy intentions and capabilities, (2) public support for risky military action, (3) consistency between diplomatic objectives and military force posture, (4) reasonable quantitative balance of strategic ends and means, (5) proper balancing between offensive and defensive capabilities, and above all, (6) predictability in threatening and using force.

The study then proceeds to offer conclusions and recommendations on the role that Anglo–French appeasement of Nazi Germany continues to play in the national security debate and on changes in U.S. force posture based on the lessons of the 1930s that remain relevant today.

Before turning to the sources of Anglo–French appeasement during the 1930s, however, it is critical to understand
the nature of both hindsight and appeasement. With respect
to hindsight, it is indisputable that Anglo–French appeasement of Nazi Germany was a horrendous mistake. However,
decision makers in London and Paris during the 1930s did
not know they were making "pre–World War II" decisions.
On the contrary, they were struggling mightily to avoid war.
We must attempt to see the security choices they faced and
the decisions they made as they saw them then, not as we
see them today. With historical events, as with football
games, it is far easier to be a Monday morning quarterback
than a Sunday afternoon quarterback in the middle of a
tough game. Nor does hindsight offer 20/20 vision; hindsight refracts past events through the lens of what followed.
Thus we view Munich today through the prism of World
War II and the Holocaust, a perspective not available in 1938.
How differently would Munich now be seen had it not been
followed by war and genocide? David Potter shrewdly observes that hindsight is "the historian's chief asset *and* his
main liability" (emphasis added).[23] Or, as Robert J. Young
notes in his examination of France and the origins of World
War II, "the problem with hindsight is that it is illuminated
more by the present than the past."[24]

As for the nature of appeasement, *Webster's New World
Dictionary and Thesaurus* defines the verb "appease" as
"to pacify, quiet, or satisfy, especially by giving into the demands of," and lists the following synonyms for the noun
"appeasement": "amends, settlement, reparation, conciliation, compromise."[25] These terms are consistent with what
most historians and international relations theorists understand to be the phenomenon of appeasement: states seeking to adjust or settle their differences by measures short of
war. Stephen Rock defines appeasement as simply "the
policy of reducing tensions with one's adversary by removing the causes of conflict and disagreement,"[26] a definition
echoed by Gordon Craig and Alexander George: "the reduction of tension between [two states] by the methodical removal of the principal causes of conflict and disagreement
between them."[27] To be sure, Anglo–French behavior toward

Nazi Germany gave appeasement such a bad name that the term is no longer usable except as a political pejorative. Before Munich, however, observes historian Paul Kennedy, "the policy of settling international . . . quarrels by admitting and satisfying grievances through rational negotiation and compromise, thereby avoiding the resort to an armed conflict which would be expensive, bloody, and possibly very dangerous" was generally viewed as "constructive, positive, and honorable."[28] Even after World War II, Winston Churchill, the great antiappeaser of Hitler, declared that appeasement could be (if driven from a position of strength as opposed to weakness) "magnanimous and noble" and perhaps "the surest and only path to world peace."

But the success or failure of appeasement depends on more than whether the appeasing state is dealing from a position of strength or weakness. Much depends on the nature and objectives of the state toward which appeasement is directed. A state bent on war or possessing territorial or ideological objectives that cannot be satisfied short of war is most unlikely to be appeasable (though it may be deterrable); conversely, a state seeking to avoid war and having limited objectives whose satisfaction does not threaten core security interests of the appeasing state is likely to be appeasable.

An oft-cited case of successful appeasement is Britain's resolution of disputes with the United States from 1896 to 1903.[29] By the 1890s the number and power of Britain's potential enemies were growing. Britain had no great power allies and faced rising imperial challenges from Germany and Russia on top of continuing traditional tensions with France and the United States. Tensions with an industrially expanding Germany became especially acute when Berlin in 1898 decided to challenge British naval supremacy in European waters. Accordingly, Britain decided to reduce the potential demands on its military power by resolving its outstanding disputes with the United States and France. With respect to the United States, it agreed to American demands that Britain explicitly accept the Monroe Doctrine; submit the British Guiana's border dispute with Venezuela to international arbitration; agree to U.S. construction, operation, and fortification of an interoceanic canal through Central America; and settle an Alaskan–Canadian border dispute in America's favor. None of these concessions involved vital British security interests, which in fact were advanced by transforming the world's greatest industrial power from a potential enemy into a friend (and later indispensable ally). Accepting American dominance within the Western Hemisphere not only laid the foundation of U.S. entry on Britain's side in World War I; it also permitted a British naval evacuation of the Western Hemisphere for operations in European waters.

But London's success with the Americans in the 1890s was not to be repeated with the Germans in the 1930s.

Why Britain and France
Appeased Hitler

ANGLO–FRENCH APPEASEMENT of Nazi Germany in the 1930s arose from multiple mutually reinforcing sources. At the forefront of those sources was memory of the Great War of 1914–18. Indeed, not much in the interwar period (1918–39) in Europe is explicable without reference at some point to the influence of World War I.

In 1914 the outbreak of war in Europe was greeted with great enthusiasm among the publics of the belligerents. The almost universal expectation was that the war would be short and decisive. War was still held to be a necessary and glorious enterprise—a relief from the "boredom" of peace and the "soulessness" of industrialization.[1] In 1939 the outbreak of World War II in Europe was nowhere greeted by the cheering crowds of 1914. Even in Germany there was no exaltation outside Nazi Party circles, only a sullen resignation. Across Europe the expectation was that the war would be long and bloody, perhaps even a repeat of the Great War. (In fact, World War II lasted two years longer and claimed perhaps 40 million more lives than World War I.)

It is difficult to underestimate the influence of the slaughter of 1914–18 on official and public opinion in Europe during the 1920s and 1930s. "Every country was affected in some way by the First World War, and its legacy hung like a shadow over international relations during the inter-war period," observes Frank McDonough. "Over 60 million Europeans fought in the war, 7 million died, and 21 million were disabled or seriously wounded. More than 4 million women lost husbands, and 8 million children lost fathers."[2] The war had an especially profound impact on opinion in the primary appeasing power of the 1930s, Britain, where vivid memories of the lost comrades and loved ones and the special horrors of trench warfare bred an electorate of which significant segments were either pacifist or unwilling to contemplate the use of force outside the authority of the League of Nations's collective-security framework. Neville Chamberlain, who became prime minister in 1937 and whose name has become synonymous with appeasement, had a simple inability to imagine that any European statesman, even Adolf Hitler, could or would wish to risk a repetition of the Great War. In the 1920s and 1930s observes P. M. H. Bell,

> it appeared to most statesmen in Britain and France that war was highly unlikely to pay. They had come to regard the last war, of 1914–18, as a calamity, involving human, material, and financial losses which should not again be incurred short of the utmost necessity. They were satisfied powers anxious to preserve the status quo; but they also wanted peace and quiet. They would eventually fight in self-defense and to prevent the status quo from being completely overthrown; but their optimism about the outcome of war was at a low ebb, and their belief in war as an instrument of policy was weak.[3]

Williamson Murray goes further:

> Any understanding of the *Weltanschauung* of [Britain's] leadership must begin with an understanding of British revulsion at the horrors of the First World War. By nature Neville Chamberlain and his colleagues were incapable of understanding the ruthlessness of men like Hitler, Mussolini, and Stalin. Nor

could the appeasers believe that their opponents on the international scene might not regard war with horror and might willingly court military confrontation and world war in order to achieve *Weltmacht*.[4]

The scale of French losses was staggering and proportionally greater than those suffered by Britain: 1.3 million soldiers dead (one-eighth of all adult males) and 4.3 million wounded (including 1.1 million with permanent disabilities). The dead left behind 600,000 widows and 750,000 orphans as well as "one-quarter of France's young women who would never find marriages and a generation to come which would be short all the children never conceived during the war and afterward."[5] For France, World War I was a demographic disaster with profound strategic implications for its continuing rivalry with a more populous and procreating Germany.

A second source of appeasement was failure to grasp the nature of the Nazi regime and Hitler's strategic ambitions. Indeed, among the sources of appeasement, misjudgment of Hitler's intentions was perhaps paramount. British leaders, most notably Chamberlain, were especially guilty on this count. Yet even after the war, the eminent British historian A. J. P. Taylor sought to prove that Hitler was a "normal" European leader practicing the opportunism of realpolitik on behalf of liberating Germany from the shackles of Versailles and restoring Germany to a political status commensurate with its population and industrial power. "Hitler was no more wicked and unscrupulous than many other contemporary statesmen." Hitler's professed ideology consisted of nothing but "day-dreams," and Hitler ended up in Russia because "his judgment was corrupted by easy victories," not because he really believed it was Germany's racial destiny to carve out massive *lebensraum* (living space) in the Slavic East.[6]

Taylor's thesis was never convincing and has been thoroughly discredited by subsequent analysis.[7] It ignored Hitler's profound nihilism and could never account for Nazi behavior in Russia or the Holocaust; more generally, the thesis willfully ignored the power of ideas in international politics.

Much of Hitler's foreign policy *was* rooted in the foreign policies of Imperial Germany and the Weimar Republic, but Hitler's racial and territorial objectives in Europe, to say nothing of his profound craving for war, lay beyond the boundaries of pre-Nazi German foreign policy.[8] Hitler's ideology defined the scope of his territorial ambitions in Europe, especially in the East, and his extermination-based racial empire was not an inheritance from Weimar or Bismarck. "The origins of this monstrous program were entirely self-generated," observes Hitler biographer Joachim Fest. "No one had ever gone to such extremes, and with such utter madness. . . . What differentiated Hitler from any conceivable predecessor was the complete lack of any sense of responsibility beyond the merely personal, of any clear-headed, selfless ethos of service, and of any historic morality."[9] What other German leader so hated the world, lusted for racial slaughter, and believed that the German people themselves deserved to perish if they failed the test of war against another race? In late November 1941 Hitler told two foreign visitors that the German people ought to "perish and . . . be annihilated" if they were "no longer strong enough and willing to shed their own blood to ensure their survival." In March 1945 Hitler told his architect and armaments minister, Albert Speer, that if the war was lost there was "no need to be concerned about the essentials the German people would need to survive even at the most primitive level" because "the [German] people have proved they are the weaker ones, and the future belongs exclusively to the stronger people in the East."[10]

To be sure, Hitler was a supreme opportunist and sought to revise the Versailles Treaty in so far as it held Germany down militarily and "imprisoned" much of the German nation outside the German state. Virtually all Germans were united in hatred of the 1919 settlement and determination to free Germany from it. But for Hitler revisionism was not an end in itself but rather an enabling precondition for action on a much larger agenda of racial conquest and enslavement. "Race, far from being a mere propagandistic slogan, was the very rock on which the Nazi Church was built," observes Norman Rich in his masterful assessment of Hitler's war aims.[11] As Margaret MacMillan notes,

> Hitler did not wage war because of the Treaty of Versailles, although he found its existence a godsend for his propaganda. Even if Germany had been left [at Versailles] with its own borders, even if it had been allowed whatever military forces it wanted, even if it had been permitted to join with Austria, he would have wanted more: the destruction of Poland, control of Czechoslovakia, above all the conquest of the Soviet Union. He would have demanded room for the German people to expand and the destruction of their enemies, whether Jews or Bolsheviks. There was nothing in the Treaty of Versailles about that.[12]

It may be hard to conceive of the possibility of Hitler without the Versailles Treaty (and the Great Depression), but Hitler was after much larger game than treaty rectification.

Hitler was hardly the first political leader to marry tactical opportunism and strategic vision, but strategic vision he manifestly possessed. Historian Gerhard Weinberg correctly believes that Hitler had "a clearly formulated set of ideas on major issues of foreign policy" and "was able to impress his ideas on events rather than allow events and realities to reshape his ideas."[13] Hitler was a racial Darwinist and his ideas centered on Aryan (Nordic) racial superiority and the imperative of carving out additional agriculturally productive lebensraum for the Aryan community between the Vistula and the Urals. Racial survival depended on racial expansion, and racial expansion depended on spacial expansion. But spacial expansion also meant inevitable war because the inferior races occupying vital living space could not be expected to voluntarily submit to the new racial order. And because war was inevitable, it necessarily became a preferred policy option rather than a measure of last resort.[14] Thus Hitler was not just another conservative German nationalist. Though many conservative nationalists supported Hitler, "Nazism went further," notes Bell.

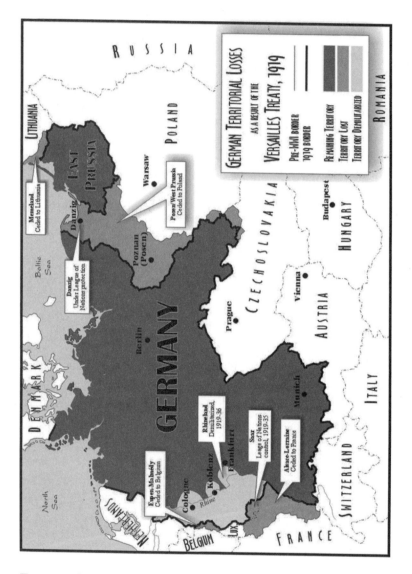

Europe after World War I

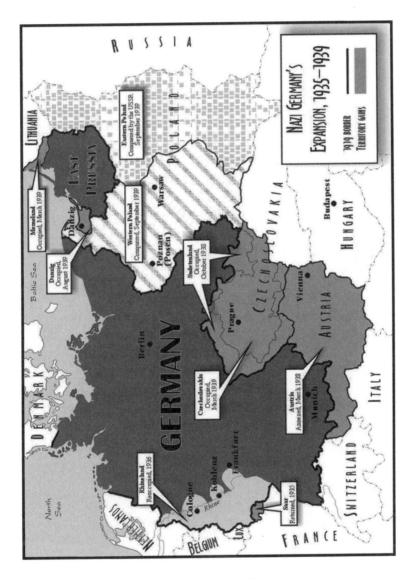

Nazi Germany's Expansion, 1936–39

The restoration of the old German Empire, even at its furthest extent, was not enough; and conservative nationalists found that their country was launched on a war of racial conquest with unlimited objectives that was almost certain to end with disaster. At different times from 1937 onwards, and with varying degrees of commitment, numbers of German conservatives parted company with the Nazi regime, though they failed to check its growing momentum.[15]

But this is all clear in hindsight—that pesky phenomenon that in this case distorts the 1930s through the lens of World War II and the Holocaust. At the time, most observers dismissed Hitler's ideological rantings on race and lebensraum as grist for domestic political consumption. The highly respected economist Dr. Hjalmar Schacht, a traditional conservative who was sacked by Hitler as minister of economics in 1937 for opposing Germany's unbridled rearmament and who was arrested and jailed in the wake of the July 20, 1944, attempt on Hitler's life, told an interviewer after the war that, during the 1920s and early 1930s, "no one took [Hitler's] anti-Semitism seriously. We thought it was a political propaganda issue and would be forgotten once he got into power."[16] Taken at face value, Hitler's vision of an Aryan empire stretching to the Urals was nothing short of fantastic; it would require the conquest of eastern Europe, destruction of the Soviet Union, and "ethnic cleansing on a grotesque scale," objectives beyond Germany's strengths and unacceptable to the European balance of power.[17] It was not difficult to dismiss Hitler's visions, which were a "strange mixture of fantasy and ice-cold calculation," as the "momentary inspirations of a runaway temperament."[18]

Ravings aside, was not treaty revision Hitler's real objective? Until March 1939, when Hitler invaded the non-Germanic rump of Czechoslovakia, it was quite plausible to believe that Hitler's military ambitions were limited to rearmament and his territorial ambitions to Germanic Europe. Most British leaders were convinced that it had been a strategic mistake to have imposed the harsh Versailles Treaty on Germany and that the treaty was in any event unenforceable; with few exceptions they "insisted on placing German aspirations within the traditional European continental balance of power, and within the system of national self-determination for all people established by [Woodrow] Wilson in 1918."[19] On this basis, Hitler *was* appeasable. Was it not ridiculous to think that Germany could be kept in a permanent state of disarmament (including the Rhineland's demilitarization) while the rest of Europe was armed? Did not Germany have a right to equality in this regard? Until 1939 Hitler's territorial demands (union with Austria and acquisition of Czechoslovakia's Sudetenland) suggested no appetite for further expansionism and its attendant risk of general war.

Indeed, Czechoslovakia itself was an affront to the principle of self-determination. Cobbled together in the name of self-determination from ashes of the Hapsburg Empire, it was less a national state than a collection of territorially based nationalities: 3.25 million Germans (concentrated in the western and northern Czech border areas with Germany), 6.5 million Czechs (in Bohemia and Moravia), about 3 million Slovaks (mostly in the eastern half of the country), plus seven hundred thousand Hungarians, five hundred thousand Ukrainians, and sixty thousand Poles.[20] The Czechs, who dominated the country's political and military leadership, were a minority in their own country. Czechoslovakia proved to be as unsustainable as the former Yugoslavia: after the cold war both jerry-rigged Hapsburg successor states disintegrated—Czechoslovakia peacefully into the successor states of the Czech Republic and Slovakia (the Russians had expelled the Sudeten Germans in 1945) and Yugoslavia in an orgy of ethnic slaughter. No British government in September 1938 would have been prepared to go to war with Germany on the wrong side of the principle of self-determination and especially on behalf of a state to which Britain had no defense obligation.

Chamberlain believed that Hitler could be sated by territorial concessions; that the dictator, like Bismarck before him, understood the limits of German power; and that he could not possibly want to plunge his country and the rest of Europe into another general war. Chamberlain did not understand, as historian Paul Kennedy notes, "that Hitler was fundamentally *unappeasable* and determined upon a future territorial order which small-scale adjustments could never satisfy."[21] More fundamentally he failed to understand, as did Winston Churchill, that the very nature of the Nazi regime barred any possibility of any long-term working strategic relationship with British democracy.[22]

That said, Chamberlain was a forceful leader who dominated his cabinet; indeed, his "dramatic offer to fly to Berchtesgaden [to meet Hitler] effectively removed from Hitler's hands the orchestration and control of the [Czech] crisis"[23] (the sixty-nine-year-old prime minister had never flown before). He was not prepared to accept a German-dominated Europe; it had long been a cardinal principle of British statecraft to align against continental powers bent on continental domination. When Hitler betrayed his promise at the Munich conference of no further territorial demands by invading the rest of Czechoslovakia in March 1939, Chamberlain and French Premier Edouard Daladier promptly extended defense guarantees to Poland, Hitler's obvious next target. The British guarantee was extraordinary because Britain was in no position to provide even indirect military assistance to Poland. The guarantee was an attempt at deterrence via the threat of general war.

Unfortunately, by the summer of 1939 the record of Anglo–French inaction over the Rhineland's remilitarization, inaction over the Austrian *Anschluss*, and the sellout of Czechoslovakia (which enjoyed a mutual defense treaty with France) had vitiated the credibility of such a threat. Hitler did not believe the British and French would go to war over Poland. In response to expressed concerns that they might, Hitler told his assembled generals on the eve of the invasion of Poland, "Our enemies are worms. I saw them at Munich."[24] Additionally, Hitler simply could not accept the possibility that the British "wanted to fight for a country they could not save."[25]

Stephen Rock, in his path-breaking assessment, *Appeasement in International Politics*, concludes that appeasement is an appropriate policy only under two basic conditions:

First, the adversary must not be unalterably committed to the behavior the appeasing state seeks to modify. The use of force, for example, if contemplated by the opponent, must be viewed as instrumental to the acquisition of a particular objective, not as an essential end in and of itself. Second, the adversary must be susceptible to inducements that is [*sic*] within the political and material capacity of the appeaser to make. If the adversary is motivated by opportunity/greed, this implies that there are limits to its demands; if motivated by insecurity, it implies that leaders are not impervious to the reassuring effects of an appeasement policy. The latter condition is most likely to be met when the adversary's insecurity is primarily a function of the appeaser's recent actions, rather than political leaders' ideology, worldview, or paranoid mentality.[26]

Against Hitler in the 1930s neither of these conditions was satisfied—or satisfiable.

Andrew Crozier reminds us that appeasement was "more than a mood: it was a practical policy designed to deal with a practical situation and was pursued by all British governments from 1919 onward. It most emphatically was not the personal property of Neville Chamberlain, although he most certainly shared in its development from 1933 onwards as chancellor of the exchequer."[27] This judgment, however, does not excuse Chamberlain's failure to grasp not only the strategic consequences of Anschluss and, above all, Czechoslovakia's dismemberment but also the consequent post-Munich imperative of some combination of an accelerated rearmament program, a firm and credible commitment to defend France and the Low Countries, and an urgent and serious exploration of alliance possibilities with the Soviet Union. By essentially writing off eastern Europe until it was too late and refusing to see that only the Soviet Union could check German power in the East while confronting Berlin with the nightmare of a two-front war, Chamberlain laid the foundations for Britain's strategic isolation in 1940–41. William Rock notes that Chamberlain, unlike other members of his cabinet, did not view appeasement as an "unhappy necessity—a choice among equals." On the contrary, he,

> insisted on seeing appeasement as a positive good. . . . The prime minister did not consider himself condemned to pursue appeasement for lack of alternatives. Rather, ascribing to Britain a kind of moral superiority by which she had risen above the factious struggles of other peoples who still groped vainly for a proper place in the European order, he thought in terms of a unique British mission to "make gentle the life of Europe." [This was] the essence of Chamberlain's appeasement.[28]

A third source of appeasement was France's military inflexibility. The French suffered fewer illusions than the British about Hitler's intentions in Europe.[29] According to historian Robert J. Young, "At no time between the wars did official quarters in France discount the possibility of a new German attack. Indeed, it was assumed that Germany would seek to crush the Third Republic as soon as Berlin detected an improvement in the military balance."[30]

Unfortunately, even before 1933 France had voluntarily stripped itself of a critical hallmark of European great power status: a willingness and capacity to attack other great powers. Indeed, next to misjudging Hitler's intentions in Europe, the second factor contributing most to appeasement was France's strategic self-paralysis. Determined to avoid the horrendous blood losses of 1914–18, alarmed by France's growing industrial and demographic inferiority to Germany, and convinced of the tactical and strategic superiority of the defense over the offense, the French General Staff by the end of the 1920s had embraced a rigid defensive military doctrine and a reserve mobilization-dependent army that precluded offensive military action into German territory.[31] The French would await a German attack behind the Maginot line, a formidable line of fortifications that conserved French manpower, while mobilizing the full strength of their army. Victory was possible, but only in a long war (as in 1914–18) in which fully mobilized French and allied resources wore down German resources to the point where centralized and methodical offensive operations against Germany became feasible. In their assessment of the French catastrophe of 1940, Eliot Cohen and John Gooch comment on the influence of the Great War in blinding the French military to the possibility that the next war might be different.

> French experiences in the First World War had burned deep into the national psyche. By 1917 the prewar French belief in the power of the offensive had been exposed as a horrible delusion as a generation of Frenchmen were sacrificed to German machine guns. In its place Pétain, the hero of Verdun, sanctified the primacy of the defensive followed by the counterattack. At war's end he came to symbolize the new military spirit of the republic, no longer relying on republican ardor and national *élan* but putting its faith in barbed wire, artillery, and concrete fortifications. The politicians of the interwar years would have found it hard to overthrow this conception of national strategy even had they wanted to, but most of them did not.[32]

The peacetime French army in metropolitan France was in fact little more than a skeleton on which the wartime force mobilized; it lacked a standing mobile strike force, and its reservists, who comprised almost half the personnel of even standing units, were poorly trained and organized. And for this state of affairs the politics of the Third Republic, not foreign policy considerations, were primarily responsible.[33] Like the American Founding Fathers, the French Left and Center had long viewed a standing army of volunteer long-service professionals as a threat to the republic itself, whereas the Right viewed an army of short-service conscripts as insufficient to guarantee social stability and the preservation of law and order. The Left and Center, which favored a conscripted national short-service army as a deterrent to military coups d'etat, prevailed on this issue in the interwar period, managing by the end of the 1920s to reduce the term of conscripted service to just one year. Conscripts were drafted for one year and then flushed into reserve components, where they did not receive adequate training. The result was an army that could not fight without general mobilization and that lacked the necessary training and cohesion to undertake large-scale and sustained offensive operations beyond its borders—an army "transformed from an active force to a potential force"[34] and one which, in the judgment of the French General Staff, was suitable only for highly centralized and methodical defensive operations.

Even absent the growth of German military power in the 1930s, France's military doctrine and strategy would have been defensive, and its army dependent on the mobilization of inadequately prepared reservists, because the politics of the Third Republic prohibited a different posture.[35] Thus Col. Charles de Gaulle's proposal in 1933—the year Hitler came to power—for the creation of a professional force of seven armored divisions (comprised of four thousand tanks, eight thousand trucks, and one hundred thousand men serving six-year tours of duty) and capable of immediate offensive operations in enemy territory was politically dead on arrival. Such a force could march on Paris as well as into the Rhineland. War Minister and Marshal Philippe Pétain and the army's senior leadership, who remained wedded to the dogma of a scripted, methodical defense that permitted little flexibility in the face of unforeseen events, also rejected de Gaulle's proposal.[36] Eugenia Kiesling summarizes the challenges of French military planning in the 1930s:

> World War I had given French soldiers a glimpse into the abyss of defeat while making them all too agonizingly conscious of the toll of survival. Their pride in victory was brittle, marred by awareness of its staggering cost, by remembered reliance on a coalition of allies, and by knowledge that France remained weaker than Germany demographically and industrially. In planning for the next war, their challenge was to protect a population with scant enthusiasm

for further sacrifices and with little faith in the leaders who would demand them. The army had to create the safest possible doctrine, one designed to win a defensive war using the short-service conscript army that French citizens were willing to provide. . . . . The doctrine of methodical battle lacked the panache of blitzkrieg, but dash had cost the French dearly in 1914, and methodical battle looked to be, if not the fastest road to victory, the safest and the surest.[37]

Nothing was inherently wrong with this defensive force posture (except the inexplicable failure of the French to extend the Maginot line along the Franco–Belgian border after the Belgians dissolved their mutual defense alliance with France). A reactive, defensive strategy, though dictated by domestic political factors and the professional military's lack of confidence in short-service conscripts for offensive combat, exploited the inherent advantages of the defense and made sense against a more powerful opponent. It also offered the only hope of exhausting Germany in a long war.

The problem was that a purely defensive military posture completely undermined France's diplomatic strategy. In seeking to deter a German attack by confronting Berlin with the prospect of a two-front war, France sought allies in the East—Russia, Poland, Czechoslovakia, Romania, and Yugoslavia—that could tie down German forces that otherwise could be thrown at France. Yet for such eastern allies, France's value as an ally depended on France's willingness and ability to attack Germany in the West, thereby tying down forces that would otherwise be available for eastern employment. Henry Kissinger observes, "None of the new states of Eastern Europe stood a chance of defending themselves against a revisionist Germany, either through their own efforts or in combination with each other. Their only hope was that France could deter German aggression by threatening to march into the Rhineland."[38] Yet as Gen. Maurice Gamelin, the chief of the French General Staff, confessed after Germany's military reoccupation of the Rhineland in 1936, "The idea of sending a French expeditionary corps into the Rhineland, even in a more or less symbolic form, is unrealistic. . . . our military system does not give us this possibility. Our active army is only the nucleus of the mobilized national army. . . . None of our units are capable of being placed instantly on a complete war footing."[39] (Interestingly, French military leaders had a clearer appreciation of the gap between France's diplomatic commitment and military capabilities than did French political leaders.[40])

During the interwar period France had created, in the words of Jean-Baptiste Duroselle, the great historian of French diplomacy during the 1930s, "*two contradictory security systems* . . . a [political] system of Eastern alliances and an alliance with Belgium . . . [and] a *defensive* [military] posture preparing a vast mobilization behind a fortified frontier."[41] Both deterrence and coercive diplomacy rest on credibly threatened force, and France lacked the political will and military capacity to make credible threats of force. French diplomacy called for a military hammer, but the French military provided only an anvil.

In this regard, Hitler's military reoccupation of the Rhineland in March 1936 was a much greater strategic disaster for the democracies than the sellout of Czechoslovakia in September 1938, but not because the Rhineland's remilitarization blocked a French attack into Germany. France, as we have seen, had no intention of attacking Germany even through an undefended Rhineland. The disaster lay in the irreparable blow to French prestige. French failure to fire a single shot at token German military forces entering territory so vital to France's security advertised France to the rest of the Continent as a feckless security partner. French inaction vindicated Belgium's decision to drop its alliance with France in favor of neutrality,[42] exposing France to the very German attack that was delivered through Belgium four years later. It encouraged Mussolini, who in thwarting a Berlin-sponsored Nazi coup in Austria two years earlier had handed Hitler a major foreign policy defeat,[43] to move closer to the German dictator. It left Austria exposed to virtually certain German annexation, thereby compromising Czechoslovakia's defense. And it undermined the eastern allies' confidence in France. The Rhineland debacle even prompted Pope Pius XI to tell the French ambassador, "Had you ordered the immediate advance of 200,000 men into the zone the Germans had occupied you would have done everyone a very great favor."[44]

But it was not just what France lost in the Rhineland; it was also what Hitler gained. Hitler later admitted that the first "forty-eight hours after the march into the Rhineland were the most nerve-racking of my life" because, if French forces had entered the Rhineland in response, "we would have had to withdraw with our tails between our legs, for the military resources at our disposal would have been wholly inadequate for even a moderate resistance."[45] As it was, concludes journalist William Shirer,

> Hitler's successful gamble in the Rhineland brought him a victory more staggering and more fatal in its immense consequences than could be comprehended at the time. At home it fortified his popularity and his power, raising them to heights which no German ruler of the past had ever enjoyed. . . . It taught [his generals] that in foreign affairs and even in military affairs his judgment was superior to theirs. They had feared that the French would fight; he knew better. And finally, and above all, the Rhineland occupation, small as it was as a military operation, opened the way, as only Hitler (and Churchill, alone, in England) seemed to realize, to vast new opportunities in a Europe which was not only shaken but whose strategic situation was irrevocably changed by the parading of three German battalions across the Rhine bridges.[46]

The foundation of French appeasement was military incapacity to act against Germany. This incapacity was strategically inexcusable, given that France was, unlike Britain, directly menaced overland by Germany, suffered fewer illusions about Nazi Germany as an enemy state, required allies in eastern Europe, possessed the largest army in Europe (upon mobilization), and was far less strategically stressed than Britain by threatened imperial defense obligations.

That said, it is important to recognize that both French and international military opinion had great confidence in the French army and considerable confidence that France could put up a stiff defense against a German invasion— that French defenses were sufficiently strong to force Germany into a protracted war that the German economy was ill prepared to sustain.[47] In April 1938 Churchill called the French army "the most perfectly trained and faithful mobile force in Europe."[48] There was a general belief in Britain and France that another world war would be a long attritional contest in which Germany would be worn down to the point of exhaustion by superior Allied resources (which in fact proved to be the case, though France became a German asset in 1940). Indeed, a war of attrition, it was believed, was the only strategy available to inflict a decisive military defeat on Germany. The stunning blitzkrieg of May–June 1940 was foreseen by no one, including the Germans, who in the event were surprised by the speed and totality of the Allied collapse. Nor was it foreseen that Hitler would conquer sufficient resources in Europe to deny Britain and France any chance of victory through attrition. Even Churchill understood, after the fall of France in June 1940, that the British Empire had no hope of defeating Hitler absent Soviet and American entry into the war (which Hitler promptly supplied in June and December 1941, respectively). Indeed, given Britain's strategic position after the fall of Dunkirk, cold-blooded realism would have dictated a settlement of the war with Germany based on London's acceptance of Germany's domination of the Continent in exchange for Berlin's guarantee of the British Empire. Interest in such a settlement was present within Churchill's cabinet in the wake of Dunkirk, and postwar historians who have sought to rehabilitate Chamberlain's reputation have argued that Churchill's decision to fight on was an egregious mistake because it doomed Britain to the loss of its empire and to postwar strategic dependence on the United States.[49]

The twin convictions that the German economy could not sustain a war of attrition and that Britain and France in alliance had a good chance of imposing such a war on Germany in the event of hostilities accounted in large measure for the lack of enthusiasm of traditional German nationalists, including senior army leaders, for any threatened or actual military action that risked general war. The convictions also underpinned the Anglo–French decision to go to war with Germany in September 1939: states are not in the habit of voluntarily entering wars they believe they will lose, and Britain and France had little reason to believe that Germany could defeat them outright. Neither London nor Paris wanted a war with Germany, but they were finally persuaded they had to fight one.

Britain's strategic overstretch was a fourth source of appeasement. While French military credibility was compromised by bad strategy, Britain's was undercut by a multiplicity of military obligations that far exceeded her capacity to fulfill them. Indeed, it is impossible to understand British defense choices in the 1930s absent recognition of a profound strategic ends-means gap arising from, on the one hand, simultaneously growing threats to Britain's security in Europe and to her imperial interests in the Mediterranean and Far East and, on the other hand, Great Depression–exacerbated constraints on the British Treasury, which severely limited funds available for defense.[50] British statesmen had long regarded Britain's financial and economic health and stability as the "fourth arm of defense"—especially in sustaining long wars of the kind Britain had waged against Napoleon and more recently against Imperial Germany, and they regarded substantial defense expenditure as a potential threat to that health and stability. Chamberlain was especially "Treasury-minded," having been chancellor of the exchequer before becoming prime minister. Thus he brought to his prime ministership not only an underestimation of the Nazi strategic threat but also a reluctance to embrace a measure of British rearmament commensurate with the rapid growth of German military power.

World War I had greatly weakened Britain's financial power by forcing London to borrow huge sums of money from the United States to cover her war costs. Though supplanted by the United States as the world's leading financial power, Britain inherited even greater imperial obligations as a result of the war's destruction of the German and Turkish empires, portions of which were transferred to Britain. Thus during the interwar period, Britain controlled a quarter of the world but accounted for but 9 to 10 percent of its manufacturing strength and war production potential.[51] This disparity between responsibility and capacity did not matter as long as Britain and its empire remained unthreatened by a major power. Indeed, British defense planning from 1919 to 1932 was based on the assumption that no major war involving Britain would arise for at least ten years. The so-called ten-year rule was a reasonable strategic guide throughout the 1920s; Germany remained weak, Japan was quiescent, and Fascist Italy was preoccupied with domestic political consolidation.

Yet as the 1930s progressed, Britain faced a rising German threat in Europe, a mounting Japanese threat in the Far East, and an expanding Italian threat in the Mediterranean—Britain's vital imperial line of communication to India and the Far East via Gibraltar, Malta, and the Suez Canal. These emerging threats—specifically, the rise of the Nazi Party in Germany, Japanese aggression in Manchuria, and Italian naval expansion—prompted abandonment of the ten-year rule in 1932.[52] What really dismayed British defense planners was the simultaneity of the threats. Against the Japanese alone, or the Germans alone, or the Italians alone, Britain could concentrate substantial fighting power. But how could Britain possibly hope to deal with all three concurrently? Small wonder that in 1935 the Committee of Imperial Defense (CID) concluded,

> We consider it to be a cardinal requirement of our national and imperial security that our foreign policy should be so conducted as to avoid . . . a situation in which we might be confronted simultaneously with the hostility, open or veiled, of Japan in the Far East, Germany in the West, and any power on the main line of communication between the two. . . . [W]e cannot foresee the time when our defense forces will be strong enough to safeguard our territory, trade

and vital interests against Germany, Italy and Japan simultaneously. We cannot, therefore, exaggerate the importance, from the point of view of Imperial defense, of any political or international action that can be taken to reduce the numbers of our potential enemies or to gain the support of potential allies.[53]

The call to reduce the numbers of Britain's potential enemies was in effect a call to appease Germany or Italy or Japan in order to free up military resources to deal with those who remained unappeased. It was a call that was hardly unreasonable, especially as the German and Japanese threats greatly worsened during the three years separating the CID assessment and the Czech crisis of September 1938. That said, British defense planners throughout the 1930s clearly recognized Germany "as the ultimate potential enemy in relation to whom long-range defense policy must be planned."[54] Even absent a German threat the possibility of a simultaneous war with Italy and Japan would stress British naval power to the point of forcing a choice between defending the empire's position in the Mediterranean or the Far East. A Defense Requirements Committee assessment in 1936 warned,

> We cannot over-emphasise the difficulties of conducting naval warfare against highly efficient enemies in two theatres so widely separated. The present troubles with Italy, which have necessitated the concentration in the Mediterranean of naval forces from all over the world, including the Far East, afford some slight indication. But it would be suicidal folly to blind our eyes to the possibility of a simultaneous or practically simultaneous threat on both fronts; and if we do not possess forces sufficient to provide a deterrent this double emergency is the more likely to occur. If there is a danger from Japan at all, it reaches its maximum from the point of view both of probability and extent when we are preoccupied in Europe. Unless we can provide a sufficient defense for that emergency, Australia, New

Zealand, India, Burma, the rich colonies East of Suez and a vast trade will be at their mercy, and the Eastern half of the British Empire might well be doomed.[55]

Chamberlain, in short, had no global military running room by the time of the Munich conference. He certainly had no means of defending Czechoslovakia or any other eastern European state not readily accessible by sea. In March 1938 the British Chiefs of Staff had submitted an assessment of the implications of a German attack on Czechoslovakia that concluded,

> [N]o military pressure we can exact by sea, or land or in the air can prevent Germany either from invading and overrunning Bohemia or inflicting a decisive defeat on the Czechoslovakian army. If politically it is deemed necessary to restore Czechoslovakia's lost integrity, this aim will entail war with Germany, and her defeat may mean a prolonged struggle. In short, we can do nothing to prevent the dog getting the bone, and we have no means of making him give it up, except by killing him by a slow process of attrition and starvation.[56]

But the issue was not simply military weakness. Military noninvolvement in eastern Europe was long-established British policy. Eastern Europe lay beyond the reach of British naval power, and London had traditionally relied upon allies in that region to provide necessary land forces. Britain was prepared to defend France and the Low Countries but not French allies in eastern Europe. Even had Britain been far better armed in September 1938 than she was, it is doubtful that London would have embraced a military solution to the Czech crisis. Chamberlain's dispute with Hitler was not over Czechoslovakia per se, but over the method of crisis resolution; the British prime minister insisted that Czechoslovakia's fate be determined by diplomacy, not force, and he was prepared to threaten the latter to achieve the former.

In 1938 Britain was not in a position to project military power east of the Rhine; the Royal Navy was preoccupied with the Italian and Japanese threats and the Royal Air Force (RAF) was in the middle of rearming. Moreover, as Richard Overy points out, Chamberlain had been prime minister for only a year and was "understandably not prepared to crown that period by deliberately courting a war that all his military advisers warned him would destroy the Empire."[57]

Britain was not even in a position to contribute to the ground defense of France and the Low Countries. The British army had no defined strategic role in the 1930s outside of home and imperial defense (at the end of 1937, 73 of the army's 138 battalions were deployed outside of Europe[58]), and it was not until February and March 1939 that the Chamberlain government concluded that a continental commitment for the British army was unavoidable and reintroduced conscription. Until 1939 the army was essentially starved to finance the expansion and modernization of the RAF, which was perceived to be Britain's first line of defense. Indeed, the one major new source of funds the army did receive was dedicated to its assigned and expanded responsibility for Britain's ground-based air defenses; the army manned Britain's antiaircraft guns during the German "Blitz" of 1940.

Until 1939 British political leaders and such influential strategic thinkers as B. H. Liddell Hart believed, or at least wanted to believe, that Britain could limit its liability in a future European war by restricting its role to the provision of naval power and airpower.[59] (During the Napoleonic era, noted Liddell Hart, Britain's main contribution to France's defeat had been sea power and the extension of financial credits to continental coalitions that provided the ground forces.) Determined to avoid a repetition of 1914–18, increasingly fearful of the German air threat (see discussion below), and persuaded that France and its Eastern allies, which from 1935 on included Czechoslovakia and nominally the Soviet Union,[60] would not require a major British ground force contribution in a war with Germany, British governments in the 1930s focused increasing defense expenditure on the RAF at the expense of the army.[61] "I cannot believe," Chamberlain confided to his diary in 1936, "that the next war, if it ever comes, will be like the last one, and I believe our resources will be more profitably employed in the air, and on the sea, than in building up great armies."[62] Openly planning for a continental war was in any event politically impossible. As chancellor of the exchequer, Chamberlain declared, "Although when the time comes [the people of this country] may, as in 1914, be persuaded that intervention by us is inevitable, they will be strongly suspicious of any preparation made in peace-time with a view to large-scale military operations on the Continent, and they will regard such preparations as likely to result in our being entangled in disputes which do not concern us."[63]

Following Czechoslovakia's dismemberment, however, the Chamberlain cabinet moved quickly toward the view that a continental commitment could no longer be avoided. Even so, not until February 1939 did Chamberlain finally authorize such a commitment in the form of two divisions within twenty-one days of the beginning of hostilities, with another two to follow within sixty-five days—drops in the bucket compared to a fully mobilized French army and a rapidly expanding German army.[64] (When war came in September, the French put 84 divisions in the field and the Germans 103.[65])

Thus, until 1939 a continental army commitment was deemed strategically unnecessary and portended a repetition of the trench warfare horrors of World War I. Furthermore, it was also believed to threaten Britain's fourth arm of defense, its economic power and financial stability, the very backbone of Britain's ability to sustain a long war for which the German economy was disadvantaged. Preservation of that power and stability and the more pressing needs of homeland air defense and naval investment combined to deny the creation of a large British army capable of holding its own against continental European adversaries.

There was, too, the problem of the empire's self-governing dominions. Canada, South Africa, Australia, and New Zealand had brought substantial resources to the British side in World War I, but their participation in another great European war could no longer be taken for granted. None of the dominions had any threatened interest in such a war unless Britain itself was attacked. They certainly had no interest in supporting a British fight over Czechoslovakia. They shared Chamberlain's view of Hitler's intentions in Europe and were greatly relieved that Chamberlain had avoided war at Munich. Japan, not Germany, threatened Australia and New Zealand; and all the dominions had a common interest in British defense spending that sustained the primacy of naval power, even at the expense of Britain's homeland air defenses. Predictably, Chamberlain did not hesitate to cite the dominions' European-war aversity to the French as a restraint on British freedom of military action,[66] but with good reason. "It would have been as preposterous as it was politically impossible for the dominions to have declared in 1938 that they would throw their armed forces into a European war," observes Michael Graham Fry.[67]

Even absent the dominions, however, London's refusal to make a continental commitment weakened British security. Such a commitment, with even a small British force deployed in northern France, would have underscored the gravity with which Britain regarded the preservation of France's territorial integrity, including the English Channel coastal regions, whose retention in Anglo–French hands would have greatly complicated any German air war against Britain. The advent of airpower afforded Germany a means of striking Britain without having to establish naval superiority in the channel and the North Sea, thus automatically inflating the strategic value of the France's channel coast and in turn increasing Britain's strategic dependence on France. If, as even Chamberlain believed, Germany was the primary European threat to British security, then an earlier and more credible continental commitment should have been made; this at the very least would have provided an army still largely mired in imperial policing duties an incentive to plan for war against Germany.

Britain's manifest strategic overstretch was a major factor in Hitler's judgment of British willingness to use force against him. Less than three weeks before Hitler invaded Poland he assured German military leaders that Britain would not fight to defend Poland. "Not even England has the money nowadays to fight a world war," he said, adding,

"England is overburdened with responsibilities because of the excessive size of her empire."[68] At a subsequent meeting Hitler again assured his senior commanders that Britain would not fight because, among other things, the British Empire was threatened around the world.

France's strategic dependence on Britain was a fifth factor behind appeasement. If Britain's acute strategic over-stretch counseled appeasement, it also propelled France along the path of appeasement because the French believed they could not act against Hitler militarily without the British in tow. France could not hope to defeat Germany by itself.

At Versailles in 1919 France had sought to guarantee its future security against Germany through a combination of mutual defense alliances with the United States and Britain and the territorial dismemberment of Germany. The realist French president Georges Clemenceau had little use for either the idealist Woodrow Wilson or his proposed League of Nations. Clemenceau wanted to preserve the wartime Anglo–French–American coalition against Germany because he believed that the events of 1914–18 had demonstrated that "without America and England, France would perhaps no longer exist."[69] He also wanted the Rhineland removed from German control via its transfer directly to France or, failing that, the establishment of a separate Rhenish state under French protection. Yet in the end neither Britain nor the United States was prepared to entangle itself in any postwar continental alliance (the U.S. Senate rejected even American membership in the League of Nations), and neither could accept the gross violation of the principle of self-determination that the forcible detachment of the Rhineland would have entailed.

French dependence on Britain was a function of Germany's growing industrial and demographic superiority over France[70] and the Nazi regime's capacity to mobilize German nationalism to a degree that the politically chaotic and decaying Third Republic never could rally French nationalism. It did not help that much of British political opinion was sympathetic to Germany's revisions of the Versailles Treaty's rearmament and territorial prohibitions. (There was much more sense of guilt over Versailles in Britain than in France, with key members of the British political elite believing that French insistence on harsh policies toward German revisionism risked provoking the very war Britain sought to avoid.) Yet, as Arthur H. Furnia points out, Versailles revisionism "permitted a rebellious Germany to augment her growing strength . . . [and] each increase in German strength made France that much more dependent upon Britain and the whims of British foreign policy."[71]

Strategic dependence on Britain was a function not only of France's relative decline vis-à-vis Germany but also of French conception of the next war and how to win it, which was shared by Britain. Given French weakness and the failure of the initial French and German offensives of 1914 to deliver a victorious short war, the French believed the next general war in Europe would be, like World War I, protracted and attritional. In such a war, victory over Germany would be possible only after years of defensive fighting during which the French and British empires (and hopefully the United States and allies east of Germany) would eventually mobilize the superior resources necessary to undertake a final strategic offensive against a Germany fatally weakened by a naval blockade and a steady loss of fighting power on the ground. This formula had delivered victory in 1918, but it also assigned enormous strategic responsibility to Britain, which with its greater financial, naval, and imperial resources brought superior long-war stamina to a conflict with Germany. Robert C. Young argues, "this was a sensible grand strategic plan, for which the French armies were generally well-equipped by May 1940." He also observes, "if German economic inferiority legitimized the concept of blitzkrieg warfare, the canon may be reversed to explain the connection between allied economic superiority and the grand strategic design of a long war."[72]

Thus France was in a bad strategic position and needed Britain; this effectively gave the British veto power over French policy toward Germany. The long-war strategy was further compromised by London's lack of appreciation of the French need for security alliances in eastern Europe, a region to which Britain was not prepared to extend security guarantees until after Munich. But the French understood that "the basic military equation in western Europe remained a France of 40 million confronted by 75 million Germans and 40 million Italians," an equation that dictated "cooperation in appeasement until the policy succeeded or until the British themselves woke up to its futility."[73]

This does not excuse France for participating in the diplomatic dismemberment of a state it was committed by treaty to defend. If France sacrificed its status as a great power by adopting a purely defensive military posture, it sacrificed its honor at Munich. Writing about the Munich conference after the war, Churchill observed, "for almost twenty years [Czech] President [Edward] Benes had been a faithful ally and almost vassal of France, always supporting French policies and French interests in the League of Nations and elsewhere. If ever there was a case of solemn obligation, it was here and now. . . . It was a portent of doom when a French government failed to keep the word of France."[74] Benes himself said, just days after Munich, "My greatest mistake in the eyes of History will be that I was too loyal to France."[75] Daladier, to his credit, felt ashamed at Munich but believed France could not defy a Chamberlain determined to sacrifice Czechoslovakia on the altar of appeasement. Daladier understood, if Chamberlain did not, the strategic and moral consequences of Czechoslovakia's sellout. "I am not proud. No, I am not proud," he told the French delegation. "The Czechs are our allies, and we have obligations to them. What I have just done betrays them. . . . The truth is that France is in a serious state. . . . What can I do if I have no one behind me?"[76]

But for both Britain and France, more than French honor was at stake. Czechoslovakia may not have been sustainable as a national state over the long run, but in 1938 it was the only democracy in central Europe and formed a significant strategic barrier to German expansion into eastern and southeastern Europe. Indeed, a major failure of British diplomacy during the road to Munich was its almost willful disregard of Czechoslovakia's formidable military capabilities.[77] During the Czech crisis of September 1938, the German army fielded thirty-seven divisions (five of them facing France) to Czechoslovakia's thirty-five divisions (plus five fortress divisions).[78] Moreover, the Czechs enjoyed three strategic advantages: they were on the defensive, operated along interior lines of communication, and possessed formidable defensive terrain and fortifications along the German–Czech border. Czechoslovakia also had the largest armaments production complex in central Europe (the Nazi takeover of Czechoslovakia in 1939 boosted Germany's arms production by 15 percent, and the arms and equipment of the disbanded Czech army were sufficient to fit out twenty new German divisions[79]).

Though most—but not all—historians believe that Germany could have beaten Czechoslovakia in 1938, there is little doubt that Czechoslovakia would have proved a much harder nut to crack in 1938 than was Poland a year later. In his assessment of the European military balance during the last two years before the war, Williamson Murray concludes that a German campaign against Czechoslovakia in September 1938 "would have involved significantly higher casualties than the campaign against Poland in 1939" because "of the nature of the terrain, the equipment of the Czech army, Czech fortifications, and the general state of unpreparedness of the German armored force."[80]

This was certainly the view of Germany's military leadership, which did not believe Germany was ready for war, had little confidence in a quick win over Czechoslovakia, and were fearful of leaving the weakly fortified Rhineland open to possible French attack.[81] Gen. Ludwig Beck, chief of the Army General Staff; his successor, Gen. Franz Halder; and Adm. Wilhelm Canaris, head of the Abwehr (the German military intelligence and counterintelligence organization) even discussed a coup against Hitler, should Hitler proceed to act on his announced decision to invade Czechoslovakia.[82] Indeed, in late August 1938 the German General Staff and Foreign Office secretly dispatched representatives to London to warn such known anti-Hitler hard-liners as Robert Vansittart and Winston Churchill of Hitler's plan to invade Czechoslovakia in September.[83] "The prime objective," concludes German historian Klaus-Jurgen Muller, was to bring about a situation in which Hitler would be forced or frightened into dropping war from his agenda. For this to happen evidence must be produced that the Western powers would oppose with armed force any further German expansion; that if war came, Germany's allies would not rally to the side of the Reich; that the German economy was not prepared for war; and finally that the desired aim could be achieved without resort to armed force.[84]

One German representative declared that German army leaders were all opposed to war "but they will not have the power to stop it unless they get encouragement and help from the outside."[85]

Interestingly, Chamberlain provided that help. In September 1938 Hitler was bent on invading and conquering all of Czechoslovakia. At the height of the crisis he declared to Sudeten leader Konrad Henlein, "Long live war—even if it lasts from two to eight years!"[86] Hitler wanted war because he was innately bloody-minded, because he sought the entire Czech state (the Sudetenland issue was a pretext), because the Czechs had embarrassed him in May by mobilizing their forces against a falsely reported imminent German attack,[87] and because in the wake of that embarrassment he had announced to his assembled generals his unalterable intention to smash Czechoslovakia. Hitler may also have wanted war because he "was keen to demonstrate to his more timid generals that he was going to be an active supreme commander. The Czech crisis was an opportunity to challenge and test the officer elite, as well as the surviving conservatives in the government."[88] Hitler was well aware of the decided lack of enthusiasm among the military leadership, the Foreign Office, and the German population at large. (Chamberlain was wildly cheered by German crowds in Munich as the real savior of peace in Europe.[89]) Mussolini was also opposed to war, as was Herman Goering.[90]

The key factor in Hitler's back down from his threat to invade Czechoslovakia was the possibility that the British and French *would* fight if Germany attacked Czechoslovakia,[91] and the key event was Hitler's meeting with Sir Horace Wilson, Chamberlain's personal emissary, on September 27.[92] Chamberlain's cabinet was divided over what amounted to a German ultimatum threatening the use of force unless Czechoslovakia accepted an immediate German takeover of the Sudetenland. Cabinet opinion was hardening against Hitler, and it decided to send Wilson to Berlin with a written plea for further negotiation and, failing that, a "special message" to be delivered orally. In "the clearest and strongest threat made by the British government during the month of the Munich crisis,"[93] that message stated, "If Germany attacked Czechoslovakia, France, as Daladier had informed us and as he had stated publicly, would fulfill her treaty obligations. If that meant that the forces of France became actively engaged in hostilities against Germany, the British Government would feel obliged to support France."[94] Hitler rejected the written plea, and the special message was then delivered. Hitler clearly understood the message to be a threat of war if he invaded Czechoslovakia, and "he clearly did not want war with the western powers."[95] According to one of Hitler's adjutants, Fritz Wiedemann, Hitler told Goering, "You see, Goering, at the last moment I thought the British fleet would shoot."[96]

The British historian Richard Overy has observed (and I agree),

> It is easy to see why Chamberlain saw Munich as a victory, and Hitler saw it as a defeat. From a position of military weakness and inferiority, with no firm allies, and an array of diplomatic imponderables, Chamberlain had almost single-handedly averted war between Germany and Czechoslovakia and compelled Hitler, for the last time, to work within the Western framework [of negotiation of territorial disputes.][97]

Hitler had sought to use the "persecution" of the German community in Czechoslovakia as a pretext for the conquest of all of Czechoslovakia; he had not foreseen Chamberlain's willingness to accept the Sudetenland's peaceful transfer to

Germany. Chamberlain had wrecked his plans. "The most disappointed man of Munich was Adolf Hitler," contends J. W. Wheeler-Bennett, author of an early work on the Munich conference. Chamberlain and Daladier "had made so wholesale a surrender of Czechoslovakia that even Adolf Hitler could not find an excuse to go to war."[98] On his return to Berlin from Munich, Hitler told Reichsbank President Hjalmar Schacht, "That fellow [Chamberlain] has spoiled my entry into Prague."[99]

Hitler regarded Munich as a defeat and came to regret allowing himself to be coerced out of war; this explains why during the Polish crisis of August 1939 he was determined not to retreat from war as he had at Munich.[100] "All his actions during the Polish crisis can be seen as a response to the defeat he felt he had suffered personally in agreeing to pull back at the end of September 1938," concludes Hitler biographer Ian Kershaw.[101] In 1945 Hitler told Martin Bormann,

> September 1938, that was the most favorable moment, when an attack carried the lowest risk for us. . . . Great Britain and France, surprised by the speed of our attack, would have done nothing, all the more since we had world opinion on our side. . . . [W]e could have settled the remaining territorial questions in Eastern Europe and the Balkans without fearing intervention from the Anglo–French powers. . . . We ourselves would have won the necessary time for our own moral and material rearmament and a second world war, even if it was altogether unavoidable, would have been postponed for years.[102]

After the war, Paul O. Schmidt, who was Hitler's interpreter and who was constantly at Hitler's side during the Nazi leader's discussions with Chamberlain, recounted Hitler's disgust at Chamberlain's popularity among ordinary Germans:

> Chamberlain was warmly welcomed at Munich. He was the hero of the German people on that occasion. It

was definitely Chamberlain who was the idol of the German people in Munich—not Hitler. The German masses gave flowers to Chamberlain. One could see on their faces that they thanked Chamberlain for saving the peace of Europe despite Hitler.

Hitler didn't like this show at all. He feared it would give the impression that the German people were pacifists, which, of course, would be unpardonable in the eyes of the Nazis. Therefore, the Nazis didn't like this Munich show at all.[103]

William Shirer was in Berlin during the Munich crisis and noted the Berliners' decided lack of enthusiasm for war. To stir up war fever among the populace, Hitler ordered a motorized division to parade through the capital; this turned into a fiasco. As Shirer recorded in his diary,

> I went out to the corner of the Linden where the column [of troops] was turning down the Wilhemstrasse, expecting to see a tremendous demonstration. I pictured the scenes I had read of in 1914 when the cheering throngs on this same street tossed flowers at the marching soldiers, and the girls ran up and kissed them. . . . But today they ducked into subways, refused to look on, and the handful that did stood at the curb in utter silence. . . . It has been the most striking demonstration against war I've ever seen.[104]

As for Chamberlain and Daladier, historian Gerhard L. Weinberg rightly stresses "the enormous significance of the circumstances in which military action is considered and the perceptions of such action at the time both by those who have to make the decision and by the segments of the public that will have to bear the burdens of any war." In this context, he concludes, "it is surprising that in the crisis over Czechoslovakia there was any serious consideration of going to war at all in Britain or France."[105]

A most intriguing if unanswerable question about Munich is, what if Czechoslovakia had decided to fight anyway? Anglo–French abandonment did not dictate Prague's renunciation of the inherent right of self-defense. The Czech military strongly favored resistance, and Churchill believed that a Czech decision to fight would have shamed France into war.[106] And who knows what might have happened then? At a minimum, Czech resistance would have bloodied Germany militarily and postponed Hitler's turn on Poland probably until the spring of 1940. Maybe his own generals would have moved against him. Moreover, as the Soviet Union was also a nominal treaty ally of Czechoslovakia, though the two states shared no common border, a fighting Czechoslovakia, especially if joined by France, almost certainly would have delayed if not altogether eliminated the emergence of any incentive on Stalin's part to cut the kind of strategic deal he made with Hitler in August 1939. President Benes's decision not to order the defense of his own country for fear that a vengeful Hitler would slaughter the Czech nation may have been a more fateful one than the Anglo–French capitulation to Hitler on the Sudetenland issue.[107] Katriel Ben-Arie believes that Czechoslovakia

> stood a fair chance of withstanding a German onslaught in September 1938, *even if she had to fight all alone*. The people were eager to fight, the generals begged Benes to resist. Even German reports spoke of a "daily gap between the actions of the government and public opinion." It was the political leadership which evinced a lack of nerve, which retreated from one position to the next, which—under ceaseless foreign pressure—conceded time and again to the demands of the Sudeten Germans, until it finally acquiesced in what was virtually the Czechoslovak republic's suicide at the end of September 1938.[108]

Looking back on France's unenviable security dilemmas at the time of Versailles conference, Henry Kissinger concludes,

France had three strategic choices: it could try to form an anti-German coalition; it could seek to partition Germany; or it could try to conciliate Germany. All attempts to form alliances failed because Great Britain and America refused and because Russia was no longer part of the equilibrium. Partitioning Germany was resisted by the same countries that rejected an alliance but on whose support in an emergency France nevertheless had to rely. And it was both too late and too early for the conciliation of Germany—too late because conciliation was incompatible with the Treaty of Versailles, too early because French public opinion was not yet ready for it.[109]

A sixth source of appeasement was guilt over the Versailles Treaty. Czechoslovakia's Sudetenland was Hitler's last territorial acquisition that could be justified on the principle of self-determination. Between his assumption of power in January 1933 and the conclusion of the Munich conference in September 1938, Hitler worked to rectify what he, all Germans, and many in Britain regarded as injustices imposed on the German state and nation by the vengeful victors of World War I. "Until 1938," observes British historian R. A. C. Parker, "British policy towards Germany was dictated by the belief among the majority of the British public that Germany had real grievances which should be rectified, grievances which derived, in large part, from the alleged follies of French foreign policy."[110]

The Treaty of Versailles indisputably was politically vindictive, economically and militarily crippling, and "widely regarded among historians, economists, politicians, and policy-makers as an unjust peace" that in turn produced "guilt feelings [that] effectively obstructed action to enforce its terms when . . . the Third Reich started casting off the treaty restrictions."[111] The treaty, signed on June 28, 1919, transferred 13 percent of Germany's prewar territory and 7 million German citizens (10 percent of Germany's total) to France, Belgium, Denmark, and the newly created states of Poland and Czechoslovakia, creating large and disaffected

German minorities in the latter two states. The treaty also prohibited any German union with Austria, the Germanic remainder of the collapsed Austro–Hungarian Empire. The treaty further stripped Germany of its colonial possessions and rights, transferring them to the victorious powers.

With respect to military power, the treaty effectively disarmed Germany. It abolished conscription; dissolved the German General Staff; limited the size of the German army to one hundred thousand men; mandated the destruction or transfer of almost all extant weapons and ammunition stocks and production facilities; prohibited the importation of war materiel; banned possession of submarines, tanks, heavy artillery, and air forces of any kind (including dirigibles); and limited the German navy to six battleships and thirty lesser vessels. The treaty also mandated the destruction of all fortifications and prohibited the introduction of any military forces on German territory to the west of a line drawn fifty kilometers to the east of the Rhine. The combination of a weak military and a demilitarized Rhineland effectively stripped Germany of any capacity to invade France—and of any defense against a French invasion.

Weakening Germany further, the treaty also imposed an immediate reparation of $5 billion and established a reparations commission that subsequently imposed an additional $33 billion in reparations. These sums, which were subsequently reduced, were well beyond Germany's ability to pay, especially given its losses in territory and population, and prompted the resignation from the British delegation of John Maynard Keynes, who quickly wrote a brilliant denunciation of the Versailles Treaty in his prescient *The Economic Consequences of the Peace*.

But perhaps the most odious of all the treaty's provisions was Article 231, which declared, "The Allied and Associated Governments affirm and Germany accepts the responsibility of Germany and her allies for causing all the loss and damage to which the Allied and Associated Governments and their nationals have been subjected as consequences of the war imposed upon them by the aggression of Germany and her allies." The so-called war guilt clause of the treaty simply added insult to injury. (To be sure, no

World War I belligerent bore more responsibility for the outbreak of hostilities in 1914 than Germany, but neither could Russia and Austria escape significant blame.)

The provisions of the Versailles Treaty were not the only source of Germany's profound humiliation. The Germans were forced to sign the treaty under the extreme duress of a continuing British naval blockade that was generating increasing starvation in Germany and a clear threat by the Allies to resume military operations against Germany. Germans rightly viewed the treaty as a punitive *Diktat* imposed at gunpoint. As such, however, the treaty proved unenforceable absent the constant threat of war by those who imposed it. The Treaty of Versailles terms "were too onerous for conciliation but not severe enough for permanent subjugation," observes Henry Kissinger. "In truth, it was not easy to strike a balance between satisfying and subjugating Germany. Having considered the prewar world order too confining, Germany was not likely to be satisfied with *any* terms available after defeat." Kissinger also notes,

> France's vulnerability and Germany's strategic advantage were both magnified by the Treaty of Versailles despite its punitive provisions. Before the war, Germany had faced strong neighbors in both the East and the West. It could not expand in either direction without encountering a major state—France, the Austro–Hungarian Empire, or Russia. But after the Treaty of Versailles, there was no longer a counterweight to Germany in the East. With France weakened, the Austro–Hungarian Empire dissolved, and Russia out of the picture for some time, there was simply no way of reconstructing the of balance of power, especially since the Anglo-Saxon powers refused to guarantee the Versailles settlement.[112]

America in fact retreated to isolationism following the Senate's rejection of the treaty, and British opinion began turning against the treaty (and against continued French belligerence toward Germany) within months after its conclusion in 1919. The British opposed risking war to enforce a treaty they believed to have been a mistake in the first place, and they believed it inevitable that Hitler would re-arm and cast off other Versailles restrictions on Germany. Hitler's demand for military equality—that is, that France and Britain should disarm down to Germany's level or Germany be permitted to rearm up to French and British levels—was difficult to counter, and once it became clear that Germany was going to rearm, Britain had a strong incentive to attempt to regulate Germany's rearmament.

Indeed, in anticipation of inevitable German rearmament that could entail a repetition of Germany's pre–World War I bid to challenge British naval supremacy in European waters, Britain cut a naval deal with Germany in 1935 that violated the Treaty of Versailles and gave Hitler a green light to start building a navy, including submarines.[113] The Anglo–German Naval Agreement, which Hitler repudiated just four years later, permitted Germany to construct tonnage up to 35 percent of that of the Royal Navy. Since Germany was starting from scratch, the agreement invited the Third Reich to build a navy as a fast as it could. The agreement, tactlessly signed by Britain on the 120th anniversary of the battle of Waterloo, shocked the French, who had not been consulted in advance, and encouraged Mussolini to believe that the British were too scared of Hitler to oppose the aggression he was about to launch in Abyssinia.[114] Indeed, Britain had not only unilaterally sanctioned a violation of the Versailles Treaty; it had also "jeopardized the security of both democracies by permitting a challenge to its own Maginot Line—the fleet."[115]

Not until March 1939, when Hitler broke the Munich agreement, did British and French policy toward Germany converge on a willingness to go to war to stop further Nazi expansion.

Keynes was hardly the only observer to conclude in 1919 that the Versailles Treaty was an invitation to another war. U.S. diplomat William C. Bullitt resigned from the U.S. delegation at the Versailles conference because he, like fellow delegate Herbert Hoover, French diplomat Paul Cambon, and South African Prime Minister Jan Smuts, believed that the treaty was a horrendous strategic mistake. British Prime

Minister David Lloyd George himself was convinced that the treaty was such a "hell-peace" that "we shall have to do the whole [war] thing over again in twenty-five years at three times the cost."[116]

A seventh source of appeasement was dread of strategic bombing and misjudgment of the Nazi air threat. Both governments and publics in Britain and France were gripped by a great fear of mass air attacks on cities, and governments misread the size and nature of the German Luftwaffe, taking at face value Hitler's announcement in 1935 that Germany already had air parity with Britain.[117] They saw in any war with Germany immediate and massive air attacks on London and Paris. (Germany had mounted significant dirigible and bomber attacks on British cities during World War I.) As early as 1921 the RAF chief of staff, Air Marshal Sir Hugh Trenchard, warned that it was "almost certain . . . a Continental Power, situated within range of our shores and engaged in fighting this country, will endeavor to end the war quickly by striking straight at our national morale through the air, rather than by circuitous, slower and more risky methods."[118] In 1928 the RAF's Air Staff informed the CID that an enemy bombing campaign against London alone would inflict twenty thousand casualties on the first night and one hundred and fifty thousand in the first week.[119]

The dread of air attack stemmed from a belief that strategic bombardment was irresistible and that its potential effects could include rapid disintegration of the political and social order. In 1932 British Prime Minister Stanley Baldwin had famously declared, "There is no power on earth that can protect [its people] from being bombed. . . . The bomber will always get through. The only defense is in offense, which means that you have to kill more women and children than the enemy if you want to save yourselves."[120] Baldwin's view was certainly the starting point for British and American airpower advocates from the early 1920s onward. The advocates believed that airpower, not armies and navies, would determine the outcome of future wars and that the best defense against air attack was a good offense in the form of massive bomber forces. They rejected investment in defenses, which (in the days before radar and "pursuit" aircraft that could fly as fast as bombers) they regarded as futile, and they were firmly opposed to diverting airpower to assist ground and naval forces.

Until the summer of 1938 the RAF remained committed to deterrence of air attack via the threat of retaliatory strategic bombardment. The persistence of this commitment was extraordinary, given the RAF's lack of bombers with sufficient range and payload to inflict more than token damage on Germany. Indeed, the strength of the RAF's ideological commitment to strategic bombing stood in stark contrast to its inability to provide convincing answers to such basic questions as what targets to bomb, how to reach them, chances of hitting them, how hard to hit them, how to determine damage inflicted, and to what effect on German morale and industry? "The RAF was, in the late 1930s," observes airpower historian Tami Davis Biddle, "an organization facing the fact that it could not carry out its own declaratory policy."[121] Interestingly, in 1937 the Chamberlain government, on the recommendation of Sir Thomas Inskip, minister for the coordination of defense (a post created to reconcile military requirements and budgetary constraints), decided to shift the RAF's funding priority from bombers to fighters. Inskip believed that British fighters in British air space could more easily destroy German bombers than could British bombers over German airfields and aircraft production sites. Fighters also were much cheaper to build than bombers, and (as it turned out) with the development of radar and the advanced Hurricane and Spitfire interceptors, Fighter Command could detect and attack the intruding German bombers.[122]

Over the strong objections of the RAF, the Chamberlain government thus opted for defense over deterrence, thereby paving the way for the victorious 1940 Battle of Britain, perhaps the most critical defensive battle of World War II.

The misreading of the Nazi air threat stemmed, first, from failure to appreciate, especially in Britain, that German airpower was being developed primarily for purposes other than strategic bombardment and, second, from deliberate strategic deception by Berlin and such influential

German dupes as Charles A. Lindberg, a pro-Nazi defeatist who trumpeted German airpower's irresistibility to British, French, and American audiences. Because the RAF "lacked adequate information on the purpose of the Luftwaffe . . . British air planners assumed that its role would not be very much different from the role they envisaged for the RAF."[123] The assumption was that Germany would attempt a "knock-out blow" against London, and as early as 1934 Churchill, a persistent purveyor of inflated estimates of German air strength,[124] argued that Germany was approaching air parity with Britain and would have three times the RAF's strength by 1937.[125] On the eve of Munich Lindberg's widely reported view was that "Germany now has the means of destroying London, Paris, and Praha [Prague] if she wishes to do so. England and France together do not have enough modern planes for effective defense."[126] (On the eve of the Munich conference British intelligence estimated that Germany had a total of 1,963 combat-ready fighters, bombers, and dive bombers, when Germany actually fielded a total of only 1,194.[127]) Bell believes that "Munich was a victory for the terror which the Germans inspired by displaying the Luftwaffe with panache, and letting their opponents' nerves do the rest."[128]

Germany in fact had nothing of the sort of air capacity Lindberg claimed. A fleet of long-range four-engine bombers lay beyond Germany's technical and industrial reach in the 1930s, and strategic bombardment was in any event alien to the kind of war the Germans planned to fight. "Luftwaffe planners, keenly aware of Germany's continental position, recognized that pursuit of an air strategy divorced from ground operations represented a luxury the Reich could not contemplate."[129] Accordingly, the Germans built an air force of relatively short-range light bombers, dive-bombers, and fighters designed to support army operations, a force whose limitations as an instrument of strategic bombardment were evident in the Battle of Britain, notwithstanding the relatively short distances separating Luftwaffe air bases in France and key targets in southern England. Nevertheless, "the misapprehension of a Germany prepared to strike a 'knock-out' blow continued right up to the war's outbreak."[130]

The French were thoroughly pessimistic about the Nazi air threat.[131] Though French intelligence correctly concluded that the Luftwaffe's primary role was to support German army operations,[132] the leadership of the French air force had no confidence in their own service in a contest with the Luftwaffe. The French air force offered Daladier no offensive options and no convincing defensive options against a sustained Luftwaffe assault.[133] Though nominally an independent service since 1930, the French air force was organizationally and doctrinally tied to the methodical defensive strategy of the French army; it had no capacity to wage a coherent air war against either the Luftwaffe or German industry. Additionally, French aircraft factories lacked mass production techniques and suffered chronic labor unrest; worse still, French air planners made premature procurement decisions that rendered much of the French air force obsolete in 1940.[134] Finally, France, like Britain, fell for Berlin's strategic deception on the strength of German airpower. A month before the Munich conference, Gen. Joseph Vuillemin, chief of the French air staff, was invited to pay the Luftwaffe an official visit. In Germany he was wined and dined, taken to air bases and aircraft production factories, and treated to "a pageant of German military power calculated to kill any French intention to use its admittedly weak air force, even though it was the only way that Czechoslovakia could be given any immediate aid."[135] The visit convinced the already pessimistic Vuillemin that the Luftwaffe could destroy the French air force in no more than two weeks.[136]

Robert Jervis argues convincingly that an exaggerated fear that "Germany would wipe out London at the start of a world war" effectively "self-deterred" Britain from taking military action against Nazi Germany until 1939. Though this fear represented a "fundamental misreading of German air policy and air strength," it nonetheless guided British decision making.[137] Moreover, as Dominic Johnson points out, an exaggerated German air threat supported the agendas of both appeasers and antiappeasers. "For the former it demonstrated that war would be very costly and should therefore be avoided; for the latter a larger Luftwaffe demonstrated that Germany had become more aggressive and therefore that the RAF must be built up to oppose it."[138]

Ironically, Chamberlain, the leading apostle of appeasement, was instrumental in setting up the RAF for its strategically critical defeat of the Luftwaffe in 1940. He not only backed Inskip's proposed shift in RAF procurement priorities from bombers to fighters, but he also, by depriving Hitler of the war the Nazi dictator so badly wanted in 1938, afforded Britain an additional year of peace with which to prepare for war in 1939. To be sure, Chamberlain did not go to Munich to buy time to rearm for a war he regarded as inevitable; in 1938 he still believed Hitler was appeasable and certainly did not regard war as unavoidable. But by threatening general war over Czechoslovakia, Chamberlain forced Hitler to back down at Munich and unknowingly gained Britain another year of fighter production and modernization (as well as a critical year for the development of a radar-based national air defense system). That additional year was crucial in the Battle of Britain. According to the official history of British rearmament in the 1930s, the RAF in September 1938 was "not . . . in a position to cope with the German Air Force," having at its disposal only six squadrons of the advanced Hurricanes and Spitfires that formed the backbone of Britain's fighter defenses in 1940. By the outbreak of the war in September 1939, the number of those squadrons had grown to twenty-six with more on the way at an accelerating pace.[139] Chamberlain, by virtue of his pre-1939 confidence in appeasement, may not have wholeheartedly accepted the necessity of the scope and tempo of rearmament from early 1937 on, but he was a firm believer in robust investment in homeland air defense.

Public opinion against war was an eighth factor encouraging appeasement. Britain's official history of its rearmament in the 1930s cautions,

> No account of the process of rearmament in Great Britain in the nineteen-thirties would be remotely correct unless it stressed, at the outset, the enormous obstacle of public unwillingness. That mood of anti-militarism which had spread over the country since 1919 was less a reasoned, intellectual conviction of the possibility of peace by international

co-operation than an emotional repugnance to the horrors and privations of war, a repugnance which had been immeasurably strengthened by the later distress of [Great Depression] unemployment. Against this no government could proceed quickly. At this stage, when not politicians but their technical advisers alone were concerned, it is important to see that even they realized that public opinion would be shocked by the revelation of what was required to place Britain's defenses on a reasonably secure footing, and admitted that the greatest care will be necessary to educate the nation as to the reasons for the heavy financial outlay involved.[140]

Not until 1939, after Hitler violently breached the Munich agreement with his invasion of the remainder of Czechoslovakia, did British and French public opinion harden against Hitler to the point where it was prepared to risk war to prevent further German expansion. Just six months earlier, both Chamberlain and Daladier had returned from Munich to cheering crowds of their respective countrymen, who were joyously relieved that war over Czechoslovakia had been avoided.

The shift in British opinion was key because of France's strategic dependence on Britain and because significant segments of the post–World War I British and French electorates were pacifist and/or committed to complete disarmament. In Britain, four years of unprecedented bloodletting in Flanders followed by a vindictive "peace" treaty convinced many that the war had been a terrible mistake and that the Versailles Treaty was not much better. Thus the famous 1933 Oxford Union vote in favor of the motion "That this House will in no circumstances fight for its King and Country." (The vote was 275 ayes to 153 nays.)[141] War phobia was particularly pronounced with respect to Germany because, as the liberal editor of the *New Statesman and Nation* observed in 1929, "Almost everyone, Conservatives, Liberals and Labour alike, regarded the French notion of keeping Germany permanently as a second-class power as absurd, and agreed that the Versailles

Treaty must be revised in Germany's favor."[142] The combination of war trauma induced by the experience of 1914–18 and sympathy toward a Versailles-wronged Germany effectively precluded any British government from carrying the country into war with Germany until Hitler clearly revealed his aggressive intentions beyond Germanic Europe. It is improbable that even the eloquent, Nazi-despising Churchill, had he been prime minister in 1938, could have mobilized public opinion for war against Hitler over the fate of Germans in a mistakenly created country that Britain was in no position to save.

The shadow of the Great War hung no less darkly over French politics. At the time of the Munich conference French veterans numbered 5 million, or 40 percent of the country's entire adult male population, and 1.5 million of them were still eligible for recall to arms as reservists.[143] A profound aversion to war was common among the peasantry, which had borne a disproportionate share of French casualties in World War I. Socialists, syndicalists, and other elements of the French Left were avowedly pacifist and antimilitarist; the French Socialist Party was committed to absolute disarmament. Even the French Right was reluctant to consider war with Germany. Pseudofascist parties and organizations despised the institutions and politics of the Third Republic, and they and the larger French Right viewed Nazi Germany as a bulwark against Bolshevism's westward spread.

The situation was not one in which British and French leaders were imprisoned by public opinion; statesmen seek to lead rather than simply follow public opinion—and both Chamberlain and Daladier were wise and experienced men in the business of government. Rather, the situation was one in which Daladier could not hope to mobilize French opinion for military action against Germany absent unambiguous British support for such action, and in which Chamberlain was still of the view that Hitler's aims in Europe were sufficiently limited to be accommodated via concession and negotiation. One could hardly expect Chamberlain to attempt to mobilize British public opinion for a war he believed was both unnecessary and avoidable—indeed, a war that he almost single-handedly thwarted at Munich via the very threat of war itself.

Unfortunately, Chamberlain, who in addition to misjudging Hitler had scant knowledge of European history or foreign affairs,[144] was determined to be his own foreign minister and brought to that task a smug confidence in his own abilities. He was not averse to changes in the European status quo that increased German power as long as those changes were not achieved by force. He knew little and cared nothing about Czechoslovakia or the rest of central and eastern Europe and regarded the Soviet Union as a pariah state. He believed his mission was to spare Europe another war and that appeasement of Germany was the path to accomplishing that mission. The veteran British cabinet officer and foreign affairs expert Leo Amery thus portrayed Chamberlain:

> Inflexibly dedicated to his self-imposed mission, he ignored the warnings of the Foreign Office, overrode wavering French ministers, brushing aside their moral compunctions as lacking realism, and, to the last moment, refused to acknowledge failure. It was only in that fixed determination that he could persuade himself, in spite of all evidence to the contrary, that Hitler's pledges were sincere, or shut his eyes to the dishonourable aspect of his treatment of the Czechs or to the worthlessness of the guarantees which he persuaded himself at the time had secured their future independence and which he afterwards cynically repudiated.[145]

The ninth source of appeasement was American isolationism. The British historian A. L. Rowse believed that "the fundamental reason for the Second World War was the withdrawal of America out of the world system: that, more than anything, enabled the aggressors to get away with things. Not all the mistakes [Britain] was responsible for in the 1920s and 1930s equaled the enormous and irreparable mistake America made in contracting out of responsibility."[146] While this hindsight suggests that it was America's duty to save

Europe from itself, there is no question that America's withdrawal from Europe's political affairs after World War I afforded Hitler a measure of strategic freedom of action he would have been denied by, for example, a firm U.S. military alliance with Britain and France.

U.S. intervention in World War I on the side of Britain and France sealed Germany's military fate in 1918, and had the United States remained politically engaged in Europe after the war, the course of events on the Continent might indeed have been different. France wanted a defensive military alliance with Britain and the United States as a deterrent to future German aggression, and had such an alliance been established and had it remained credible (via perhaps the forward deployment of British and American combat forces in France), it is difficult to imagine Hitler courting war with the great coalition that had defeated imperial Germany. Hitler, who sought to dominate the entire continent, might have been compelled to settle initially for a German empire confined to eastern Europe and Russia, and perhaps only then turning on France.

Norman Rich, in his assessment of the reasoning behind Hitler's fatal declaration of war on the United States following the Japanese attack on Pearl Harbor, contends that Hitler expressed contempt for American military capabilities "to instill courage in people justifiably fearful about America's strength," but nonetheless pursued pre–Pearl Harbor policies toward the United States that were "determined by a very realistic respect for American power and by a constant fear that America might intervene in the war before Germany's position on the European continent had been consolidated."[147] Until the Japanese attack on Pearl Harbor, Hitler was careful not to provoke war with an increasingly belligerent Franklin Roosevelt because he was greatly impressed with America's sheer size and capacity for mass production.[148] (His views on America's racial composition were another matter.)

America of course absented itself from Europe's political affairs during the interwar period. It took World War II and the postwar emergence of the Soviet threat to convince most Americans that the key to avoiding entanglement in yet another European war was to establish peacetime military alliances with threatened states. Roosevelt, who from the beginning had reservations about the wisdom of Chamberlain's policy of appeasement, grasped the nature and severity of the Nazi threat long before he was politically able to do much about it. By the end of 1937 he was persuaded that the Anti-Comintern Pact between Germany, Japan, and Italy constituted a secret offensive-defensive alliance aimed at world conquest, and though he subsequently flirted with appeasement because Chamberlain seemed committed to it, the Munich agreement and the bloody November 1938 Nazi anti-Jewish pogrom known as *Kristallnacht* disabused Roosevelt of any further doubt that Hitler's aims were unlimited and that Nazi Germany could be stopped only by credibly threatened force.[149]

Roosevelt's freedom of action, however, was severely limited by a decidedly isolationist Congress. The Neutrality Act of 1937 prohibited the United States from supplying arms or extending any loans or credits to any belligerent in a European war. Because the act made no distinction between aggressor states and their victims, it blocked Roosevelt from assisting Europe's democracies if they were attacked by Nazi Germany and Fascist Italy. In so doing, it eliminated the possibility of credible American threats to participate in the strategic containment of Hitler and Mussolini. It is testimony to the isolationists' grip on Congress (as well as to Capitol Hill's determination to reverse what it saw as a growing executive branch accretion of power at the expense of the legislative branch[150]) that the Senate rejected Roosevelt's personal pleas to loosen the provisions of the Neutrality Act until after war broke out in Europe in September 1939 and did not repeal the key provisions of the act until the eve of Pearl Harbor. Indeed, Congress did not authorize conscription until September 1940—after the fall of France and the Low Countries, and amazingly, the House of Representatives voted to renew authorization for conscription by only one vote in August 1941—two months after Hitler invaded the Soviet Union and only four months before Pearl Harbor.

Even had the Neutrality Act been defeated in 1937 (the

year Chamberlain became prime minister), the United States could hardly have acted against Hitler when no one else in Europe would. While public opinion in Britain and France blocked political decision makers from risking war to stop Hitler until it was too late, a tradition of isolationism from Europe's wars and the seeming remoteness of the German menace to America and its Western Hemispheric security interests virtually precluded war against Germany absent a German attack or declaration of war. C. A. MacDonald summarizes Roosevelt's dilemma:

> It was difficult to persuade [American] public opinion that an axis danger existed while Chamberlain continued to talk about an Anglo–German agreement. Yet Roosevelt could not persuade Britain to take a stiffer line with Germany without widespread support for an anti-axis policy which would convince London that American support would be quickly forthcoming in the event of war. The President was caught between the desire to play a larger role in world affairs and the necessity of preserving his political position at home. He never solved the problem of balancing these two factors. While public opinion increasingly supported an active anti-axis policy after September 1939, it never reached the point of endorsing American military intervention.[151]

Roosevelt, beginning with his famous October 1937 "Quarantine Speech" (which was roundly denounced by isolationists) in Chicago, began a campaign to educate the American people on the gathering threat posed by the fascist dictators in Europe and Imperial Japan. And beginning in 1938 Roosevelt, who was an airpower enthusiast and believer in a potential German air threat to the Western Hemisphere, started a campaign to rearm the United States, focusing primarily on expanded naval power and airpower. Munich convinced Roosevelt that Hitler could never be trusted and that Germany would eventually threaten the United States.[152] From the outbreak of war in Europe in September 1939 to the Japanese attack on Pearl Harbor in

December 1941, Roosevelt transformed the United States from a rigidly neutral bystander into a provider of war assistance (Lend Lease) to Britain (and after September 1941 to the Soviet Union) and a de facto naval cobelligerent with Britain against the German submarine menace in the North Atlantic.[153]

Woodrow Wilson had told his fellow countrymen that America's entry into the Great War was necessary to make the world safe for democracy and that indeed the struggle would put an end to war itself. He then joined France and Britain in imposing a punitive peace on Germany that neither Britain nor the United States was prepared to enforce and which crippled prospects for enduring democracy in Germany. A petulant and uncompromising Wilson went on to ensure Senate defeat of U.S. membership in the League of Nations, which crippled prospects for effective collective security against fascism and militarism. Little wonder that most Americans wanted to have nothing to do with another European war.

The last but by no means least factor contributing to appeasement was distrust of the Soviet Union and fear of Communism. The alternative to appeasement of Hitler in the 1930s was the formation of the kind of grand alliance that crushed Nazi Germany 1945. This alternative, however, was never more than theoretical until Hitler invaded the Soviet Union in June 1941 and declared war on the United States the following December. Domestic politics precluded war or military alliance with threatened states in Europe as voluntary policy choices for the United States. But this was not the case for the Soviet Union, which Hitler both reviled and targeted for German racial expansion. Stalin clearly understood Nazi Germany for the deadly foe it was, and in 1934 the Soviet Union entered an alliance with France as a means of checking German expansionism. Russia and France had been close allies against Imperial Germany, and the Soviet Union in the 1930s constituted the only great power east of Germany. It fielded the largest standing army in Europe and possessed war production potential second only to that of the United States. The same logic that underlay the Anglo–French–Russian alliance of World War I against Imperial Germany applied to stopping Hitler from plunging Europe into another world war, and this logic should have been glaringly apparent after Hitler removed any doubt over his trustworthiness and territorial intentions by invading what remained of Czechoslovakia after Munich.

Yet in August 1939 Stalin entered a nonaggression pact with Hitler that essentially freed German forces, once they (in conjunction with Soviet forces) had erased Poland, to attack in the West with no fear of having to wage war on a second front in the East. Stalin's conversion from a potential ally of the West into a collaborator with Nazi Germany was the product of several factors, but primary among them was Anglo–French appeasement of Hitler and manifest fear and mistrust of the Soviet Union and its dreaded gospel of Communism. Many Britons and Frenchmen believed Communism posed a greater threat to the West than Nazism did, and there were in any event reasonable doubts about the Soviet Union's value as an ally against Hitler, especially after Stalin murdered the professional heart of the Red Army officer corps in 1937–38. "It was natural for European states, especially the great imperial powers, Britain and France, to regard Soviet communism as their sworn enemy—for so it was," observes Bell. "From this fact of life some took the short step to the belief that the enemies of communism were your friends, and that fascist Italy and Nazi Germany were useful bulwarks against Soviet influence. Once this notion took root, it was hard to accept that the Nazi regime was itself a threat, nearer and more dangerous than the Soviet Union."[154]

Hitler was also in a position to offer Stalin extensive territorial concessions east of the Vistula River that Britain and France could not. The nonaggression pact contained a secret protocol that granted Stalin the eastern half of Poland, conceded to the Soviet Union a free hand in Finland, Estonia, and Latvia, and recognized Moscow's interest in the Romanian province of Bessarabia. Under the circumstances, and given the Anglo–French record of appeasing Hitler, Stalin's choice of a deal with Hitler rather than an alliance with Britain and France was hardly an agonizing one. Andrew Crozier has summed up the array of considerations as they appeared to Moscow.

> Did the Western powers really intend to resist Hitler? And, if they did, were they capable of doing so effectively? If the answer to either of these questions was even vaguely negative, the Soviet Union, through too close an association with the democracies, could have found herself at war with Germany without credible allies in the west. This would have been particularly embarrassing militarily for in 1939 a state of undeclared war existed between the USSR and Japan in the Far East which might ultimately have resulted in a debilitating war on two fronts. On the other hand, the German offer was very attractive. It certainly meant the postponement of war from the Soviet point of view; it implied the possibility of being able to emerge as the *tertius gaudens* from a conflict between the capitalist powers; and [it] allowed the extension of the USSR's defensive lines into Eastern Europe and the Baltic littoral. Stalin opted for the certainties of an accommodation with Hitler, rather than the uncertainties of a tie with Britain and France.[155]

A grand alliance with the Soviet Union in peacetime was simply not in the diplomatic cards until 1941. Aside from British and French (and American) professional military reservations about the quality of the horrendously purged Red Army, much of Britain's ruling class and almost all of France's senior military officers were profoundly hostile to Communism—and by extension to the Soviet Union, the world's only Communist state in the 1930s. The French had a 1934 defense treaty with the Soviet Union, but it had never been consummated via military staff talks.

> In particular, what especially offended French officers and politicians alike," observes Robert J. Young, "was the activity of Moscow-inspired propagandists

in local election constituencies and military barracks. Closer contact with Moscow, especially on the part of staff officers, was regarded as something akin to exposing them to a communicable disease, the severity of which could not be predicted with confidence. . . . [Many senior officers also] believed . . . that closer [French] association with Russia could injure relations with England and thus put paid to the eternal hope of securing closer military cooperation with Great Britain.[156]

As for the British, an assessment by Donald N. Lammers convincingly concludes that a desire to destroy Russia or to see Russia destroyed by Germany played no active or even passive role in British calculations with respect to Nazi Germany, which London clearly understood was the greatest threat to British security and the peace of Europe.[157] Nonetheless, Chamberlain's innate anti-Soviet revulsion inhibited a timely recognition that the Soviet Union offered the only means of confronting Hitler with the threat of a two-front war.

Anglo–French appeasement of Nazi Germany during the 1930s was the product of multiple political, military, and psychological factors that combined to deny any realistic possibility that the Western democracies could or would act effectively against Hitler in time to thwart outbreak of a second world war in Europe. This is not to embrace historical determinism; rather it is simply to argue that the alignment of political, military, and psychological factors in the 1930s was never such as to offer both London and Paris simultaneously a clear appreciation of the nature and scope of the German threat as well as the opportunity to employ military force confidently and effectively against that threat. In hindsight condemning appeasement because it led to World War II is easy, but until 1939 the record of appeasement was one sparing Europe *from* war. Chamberlain and Daladier could not know they were making pre–World War II decisions; on the contrary, they were struggling to avoid war—but *not* at any cost. When in 1939 Hitler violated the Munich agreement and in so doing dispelled any lingering doubts in London and Paris about his real intentions in Europe, Chamberlain and Daladier committed to a policy of war by extending defense guarantees to Poland and other threatened states.

Diplomatic choices for London and Paris in the 1930s were neither obvious nor easy. Robert J. Beck has insightfully summarized the dilemma-ridden maze that confronted British statecraft during the period:

> Given a strong hand, the diplomat's task is comparatively uncomplicated: at times even a bumbler may prevail. Should the diplomat face a lesser opponent while holding a poor hand himself, he may still win if he plays skillfully. If, however, his opponent is crafty and his own hand seems mediocre, the challenge before him is daunting: if the diplomat's judgment is faulty, disaster is virtually certain.
>
> . . . [T]his was the unhappy situation faced by Neville Chamberlain in September of 1938. Adolf Hitler was exceedingly shrewd and inscrutable, a master of bluff and deception. The German leader held an ace card, his claim to be the champion of *Sudetendeutche* 'self-determination.' And in the event his opponents proved uncooperative, Hitler prominently displayed an intimidating weapon, the German military. By contrast, Chamberlain's hand appeared rather weak indeed: Britain could not rely upon American military assistance in the event of war; the Dominions seemed divided on the Czech question; if a European war came, Japan might seize the opportunity for expansion; there were signs that the public might not support a war with Germany; and perhaps most disturbing, the British military had argued that it was ill-prepared for a major confrontation. In short, Chamberlain's position seemed perilous.[158]

Why Appeasement Failed

EXPLANATIONS OF HISTORICAL EVENTS, such as Anglo–French appeasement of Nazi Germany, are rarely simple or self-evident. Explaining appeasement's failure is an exception. Anglo–French appeasement of Adolf Hitler failed simply because Hitler was unappeasable. He wanted more, much more, than Britain or France could or would give him. Neville Chamberlain sought to propitiate Germany within the framework of Europe's traditional power system; Hitler sought to overthrow that system. He fooled Chamberlain (and many others in Europe, including traditional conservative German nationalists) into believing that Nazi Germany's foreign policy ambitions, like those of the Weimar Republic, were limited to rectification of the "injustices" of the Versailles Treaty, and until 1939 he was careful to limit Germany's explicit territorial demands to Germanic Europe, demands he justified in the name of national self-determination. In this regard, British policy toward Germany was consistent from 1919 on: it sought to bring "Germany back into the community of nations . . . negotiating the relaxation of those [Versailles] treaty restrictions that were perceived as untenable." London "never supported the French policy of enforcing the Treaty of Versailles or the French system of alliance with Eastern Europe."[1] Needless to say, the success of Hitler's diplomacy in the 1930s profited immensely from basic Anglo–French differences over how to deal with Germany.

To be sure, Hitler was not shy about discussing the scope of his ambitions in Europe. *Mein Kampf*, which Hitler wrote while in prison ten years before he came to power, might be dismissed as the rantings of a failed revolutionary, but once in power, the Nazis' innate savagery and Chancellor Hitler's numerous public declarations of Germany's racial destiny in the Slavic East, the imperative of Aryan seizure of *lebensraum* in the vast domain of the inferior races that lay between Germany and the Urals, could not be so easily ignored. As Norman Rich notes, what Hitler had in mind as a model was not the Hapsburgian one of "indiscriminate annexation of peoples of different races and religions," but rather "that of the Nordics of North America who swept aside lesser races to ensure their own ethnic survival."[2] But was this not a literally fantastic vision? How would Hitler go about it? Would eastern Europe and Russia submit? Would the rest of Europe accept a continental German empire that would destroy the European balance of power? Was any head of a major European state really prepared to plunge the Continent into another bloodbath on behalf of a crackpot racial theory? It all seemed incredible.

The very fact that Chamberlain could not bring himself to believe that Hitler wanted another world war testified to his understanding that any German bid for continental domination meant war, and in 1939 Chamberlain was even prepared to—and did—go to war with Germany for the sake of a country Britain was in no position to defend. Hitler, and ultimately Chamberlain, understood that his imperial ambitions in Europe could not be satisfied without war. Chamberlain, in contrast to his successor, Winston Churchill, was not only misled by Hitler but also poorly versed in European history and the realities of international politics, but even he understood, as had his predecessors during the Napoleonic era, that a Continent dominated by a single hostile power threatened Britain's survival as a sovereign state.

But Hitler was not just unappeasable. He was also *undeterrable*. And it was this undeterrability that made

Hitler so dangerous. True, shows of strength and resolve—Mussolini's reaction to Hitler's attempted Nazi coup in Vienna in 1934, Britain's "special message" of September 1938 that it was prepared to join France in going to war over Czechoslovakia—forced Hitler to back off. But he did so only because Germany was still rearming and Hitler was not yet prepared to risk military defeat or a general war. Also true, Hitler planned for general war no later than 1943–45, when he believed Germany would attain maximum power relative to her enemies,[3] and was surprised when the French and British prematurely visited it upon him in 1939 by honoring their defense guarantees to Poland. (Hitler mistakenly assumed not only that his nonaggression pact with the Soviet Union would deter the West from going to war over Poland but also that Italy would honor its alliance with Germany in the event of general war; he was flabbergasted, to the point of temporarily postponing his attack on Poland, when Mussolini informed him that Italy was not ready for war.[4]) But Hitler's major miscalculation of British, French, and Italian responses to his imminent attack in no way affected pursuit of his long-term racial objectives in the East. J. L. Richardson properly sums it up. Given Hitler's ideologically driven expansionism,

> it follows that neither appeasement nor deterrence could have succeeded in averting war. The fundamental reason for the failure of appeasement was that Hitler's goals lay far beyond the limits of reasonable accommodation that the appeasers were prepared to contemplate. If appeasement encouraged him to increase his demands, it was only in a short-term, tactical sense. Likewise, if a policy of deterrence or firmness had been adopted earlier, it would have changed Hitler's tactical calculations, but there is no reason to suppose that he would have modified his goals.[5]

War was thus inevitable as long as Hitler remained in power. Clearly, the appeasers had illusions about Hitler, but no less clearly, as Ernest R. May observes, "'Anti-appeasers' had their own illusions which were almost equally distant from reality. They believed that Hitler could be deterred by the threat of war. Few suspected that Hitler *wanted* war."[6] The threat of war cannot be expected to scare off a regime that welcomes war. In this regard, Hitler was fundamentally different from Stalin. Stalin was patient and cautious, his ambitions in Europe were limited, and he responded to credible deterrence.

Hitler's undeterrability renders moot much discussion about what might have been. Would, for example, a credible Anglo–French alliance with the Soviet Union have deterred Hitler from seeking to subdue the Slavic *untermensch* in the East? Hitler was ideologically predestined to invade the Soviet Union, for which he had both racial and military contempt, and he proceeded to do so in June 1941 notwithstanding an unfinished and expanding war with Britain in the West and the growing difficulties of his Italian ally in the Balkans and the Mediterranean. There was, of course, virtually no prospect of a credible Anglo–French–Soviet alliance. Most of British and much of French political opinion was extremely hostile to Bolshevism and the Soviet pariah state; an alliance with Moscow would be a pact with the Devil. Indeed, a significant segment of French opinion preferred a Fascist political order in France itself and viewed Nazi Germany as an indispensable barrier to the westward spread of Bolshevism. Russia's military value as an ally was also questionable, especially after Stalin's decimation of the Red Army's senior leadership. Nor did the Soviet Union share a border with Germany; thus Moscow could not project military power against Germany except through Poland and Czechoslovakia.

The *combination* of Hitler's unappeasability and undeterrability meant that war could have been avoided only via Hitler's death or removal of from power, options apparently not considered by London or Paris and only briefly weighed by some German military leaders in 1938. Beyond Hitler's departure from power, only a preventive war that crippled German military power, collapsed the Nazi regime, or both could have averted World War II. Given the horrors of that war, initiation of a preventive war seems retrospectively imperative, and when neoconservatives such as Richard Perle speak about how Hitler could and should have been stopped before 1939, they mean via forcible regime change of precisely the kind the United States launched against Iraq in 2003. But it is here that the neoconservatives enter the fantasy realm of historical counterfactualism. For Britain and France in the 1930s, a decisive preventive war against Germany was morally unacceptable, politically impossible, and militarily infeasible. Rewriting history is always easier than writing it. If Chamberlain horribly misread Hitler, the neoconservative indictment of Chamberlain conveniently assumes that the option of preventive war against Germany was as available to London and Paris in 1938 as it was to the United States against Iraq in 2003.

The American experience in Iraq testifies to the perils inherent in forcible regime change, especially forcible regime change undertaken on the basis of rosy neoconservative assumptions about the degree of difficulty involved and without adequate preparation for the possibility of postregime violence and the challenges of national political and economic reconstruction. Yet one can speculate that the magnitude of the task of forcible regime change in Germany in, say, 1938 would have dwarfed that in Iraq today. Hitler was a genuinely popular leader within Germany, whereas Saddam Hussein was detested by all but the minority Sunni Arab population. Germany in 1938 had a burgeoning economy and a rapidly expanding and highly competitive military establishment, which could have been counted upon to offer much more formidable resistance than Saddam's sanction-crippled forces. An effective occupation and reconstruction of Germany would in any event have required far more manpower, resources, and time than the United States has been prepared to invest in Iraq.

Germany without Hitler almost certainly would have been deterrable, and indeed it is hard to see how Europe gets to World War II without Hitler. Any German government of the 1930s would have pursued rectification of the Versailles Treaty injustices, but even a government of traditional conservative nationalists of the kind that Hitler discarded on his road to war (precisely because they opposed his reckless policies) would have respected the limits of German power and the unacceptability to Britain and France of a German-dominated Europe. Such a government would have been happy to recover lost German territory in Poland, even to see Poland disappear, and perhaps might have dreamed of another Treaty of Brest-Litovsk—but not at the cost of general war for which Germany was not prepared (the German economy was not placed on a total war footing until 1942). Almost certainly there would have been no slaughter of Jews.

Appeasement's Lessons for the United States Today

DOES ANGLO–FRENCH APPEASEMENT of Nazi Germany offer strategic lessons of value to the United States today, and if so, what are those lessons?

The strategic environment of the 1930s—imperial, Eurocentric, dominated by great power rivalry—bears little comparison to today's globalized environment of both state and nonstate actors in which a single "hyperpower" enjoys worldwide conventional military primacy. Imperial collapse—European colonial followed by Soviet Communist—has flooded the international system with over one hundred new states. Lesser wars against unconventional enemies have largely displaced big conventional wars between states. Weak and failed states have supplanted great powers as the primary source of security threats. Europe, for centuries a cockpit of war, has become a zone of seemingly perpetual peace. The United States, a military pygmy, self-isolated from Europe's politics in the 1930s, has become a military giant and the capstone of a worldwide network of formal and informal political alliances. The Soviet Union, the great object of Hitler's ambitions and the primary source of Nazi Germany's destruction, has disappeared.

Statesmen of the 1930s could not possibly have imagined the strategic landscape of the first decade of the twenty-first century. That said, the 1930s provide important lessons for today's statesmen in addition to the one that is so obvious in retrospect: Don't propitiate an insatiable great power dictator if you are in a position to pursue an alternative policy. The trick, of course, is to recognize insatiability and to have at hand the will, wherewithal, and opportunity to deter and defeat rather than appease.

The first "other" lesson, though hardly unique to the 1930s, is that threat miscalculation can have severe penalties. Dominic Johnson, in his study *Overconfidence and War: The Havoc and Glory of Positive Illusions*, notes that Neville Chamberlain simultaneously underestimated Adolf Hitler's intentions and overestimated the German military threat to Britain. Chamberlain believed that Hitler's objectives in Europe were limited, but he also believed that "we cannot expose ourselves . . . to a German [air] attack. We simply commit suicide if we do. At no time could we stand up against German air bombing."[1] War with Germany thus not only *could* be avoided but also *had* to be avoided.

War is the province of miscalculation. History is littered with wars arising from misperceived enemy intentions, capabilities, or both, and this reality seems endemic in the practice of statecraft. Just as Chamberlain misread Hitler's intentions in 1938, Hitler misread British intentions in 1939. In Korea in 1950, the Soviets misread the intentions of the Americans, who in turn misread the intentions (and capabilities) of the Chinese. In Vietnam, the United States overestimated its own capabilities and underestimated those of the Communists. And Saddam Hussein misread George H. W. Bush's intentions in the Persian Gulf in 1990–91, while the George W. Bush administration misread Saddam Hussein's capabilities as it approached America's second war against Iraq in 2003. Saddam certainly wanted deliverable weapons of mass destruction (WMD), but wanting is not the same thing as having.

The failure to discover chemical and biological weapons and programs to develop nuclear weapons in the aftermath of a war waged against Iraq in large measure because those weapons and programs were presumed to exist greatly embarrassed the United States and called into question the quality of its very expensive intelligence-gathering community. If that community could be wrong about Iraq's supposed WMD, could it not also be wrong about the WMD status of other so-called rogue states? Even if it is assumed that policymakers neither pressured the community to come up with intelligence supportive of military action against Iraq nor "cherry-picked" pro-war bits of information from intelligence data, the intelligence community itself stands convicted of an intelligence failure worse than that preceding the attack on Pearl Harbor.[2] (The surprise of December 7, 1941, was not a Japanese attack on U.S. forces in the Pacific, but its locus. Intercepted secret Japanese communications had alerted Franklin Roosevelt and the War and Navy departments to the imminence of an attack, and final war warnings were transmitted to U.S. commanders in the Pacific ten days before the Japanese struck. It was assumed, however, that the Philippines, not Pearl Harbor, would be the target. Both were in fact attacked.)

The 2005 report of a presidential commission on U.S. intelligence capabilities regarding WMD was blunt in its assessment.

> We conclude that the Intelligence Community was dead wrong in almost all of its pre-war judgments about Iraq's weapons of mass destruction. This was a major intelligence failure. Its principal causes were the Intelligence Community's inability to collect good information about Iraq's WMD programs, serious errors in analyzing what information it could gather, and a failure to make clear just how much of its analysis was based on assumptions, rather than good evidence. On a matter of this importance, we simply cannot afford failures of this magnitude.[3]

The commission elaborated on the sources of failure.

> This failure was in large part the result of analytical shortcomings: intelligence analysts were too wedded to their assumptions about Saddam's intentions. But it was also a failure on the part of those who

collect intelligence—CIA's and the Defense Intelligence Agency's (DIA) spies, the National Security Agency (NSA) eavesdroppers, and the National Geospatial-Intelligence Agency's (NGA) imagery experts. In the end, those agencies collected precious little intelligence for the analysts to analyze, and much of what they did collect was either worthless or misleading. Finally, it was a failure to communicate effectively with policymakers; the Intelligence Community didn't adequately explain just how little good intelligence it had—or how much its assessments were driven by assumptions and inferences rather than concrete evidence.[4]

Worse still:

The flaws we found in the Intelligence Community's Iraq performance are still all too common. Across the board, the Intelligence Community knows disturbingly little about the nuclear programs of many of the world's most dangerous actors. In some cases, it knows less than it did five or ten years ago. As for biological weapons, despite years of presidential concern, the Intelligence Community has struggled to address this threat.[5]

It is beyond the purview of this study to propose reforms in the intelligence community, though there seems to be a consensus on two deficiencies that need to be remedied: (1) inadequate communication and information sharing among the various agencies that comprise the intelligence community and (2) an inexcusable dearth of human intelligence sources. Both the Commission on the Intelligence Capabilities of the United States Regarding Weapons of Mass Destruction and the National Commission of Terrorist Attacks on the United States (known as the 9/11 Commission) have recommended major changes in the ways in which the community is organized and does business.[6] The question nevertheless remains: If such a large and technically proficient intelligence community could be "dead wrong" about so seemingly simple a matter as the presence or absence of WMD in a state that had been under intense surveillance for thirteen years, on what basis can there be any confidence that the community will get it close to right in assessing the WMD status of other hostile states? In the 1930s Germany's rapid rearmament was hardly secret; rearmament was visible—indeed, Hitler openly boasted of it to the point of strategically deceiving Britain and France into believing they faced an earlier and greater threat than was actually the case. With respect to Iraqi WMD, the threat was presumed on the basis of postulated Iraqi intentions and the assumed continued existence of residual WMD stocks and materials unaccounted for by international inspection regimes.

What has become known as the Bush Doctrine calls for taking anticipatory military action against emerging threats before those threats fully mature; as such, the doctrine is firmly rooted in the perceived great strategic lesson of the 1930s—namely, that World War II could have been avoided if the Western democracies had used force early and decisively against Hitler. The utility of the Bush Doctrine, however, is contingent upon an ability to identify the presence, strength, and direction of emerging threats. Inability to do so invites war via miscalculation.

A second pertinent lesson of the 1930s is its reminder that democratic governments are constrained by public opinion. The fact that both Neville Chamberlain and Edouard Daladier were wildly cheered by crowds on their return from Munich testifies to the domestic political impossibility of an Anglo–French decision for war over Czechoslovakia in September 1938. Leaders of democratic states must necessarily consider public opinion in making decisions to use (or not use) force. They can and do attempt to mobilize public opinion for war, but in the end they cannot readily march off to major war—or continue to sustain a policy of war—in the face of a hostile electorate. This is especially the case in wars of choice as opposed to wars of necessity. The vast majority of America's wars have been wars of choice even though most have been sold to the electorate as wars of necessity. Indeed, mobilizing American

public opinion for war virtually dictates presidential asser-
tions of necessity (threatened core security interests, the
moral imperative for action, or both) and accounts for the
attractiveness of the Munich analogy as a White House tool
for mobilizing public opinion. No president is going to say,
"The war I'm contemplating is not really necessary, but I'm
going to fight anyway." The president instead will say, "We
have no choice but to act."

To be sure, neither Chamberlain nor Daladier attempted to mobilize their respective electorates for war;
Chamberlain believed war could be avoided, and Daladier
believed France could not fight without Britain at her side.
But even had Chamberlain been convinced that Britain had
to fight in 1938 to prevent Czechoslovakia's dismemberment, it is difficult to see how he could have rallied the
British public behind him.

For a democratic government, mobilizing public opinion for a major use of force is but the first challenge. The
second and often more difficult challenge is that of sustaining support once war has begun. Much depends on the quality of that government's political leadership, the course and
duration of hostilities, and the electorate's perception of the
stakes at issue. Sustaining public support is especially difficult in protracted wars against irregular enemies capable of
stalemating the fighting and in which the accumulating war
costs are seen to exceed benefits of military success.[7] Such
was the case in the Korean War and even more so in the
Vietnam War. U.S. public support for both steadily declined
as casualties rose, as a decisive military victory came to be
seen as beyond reach, and as the stakes no longer appeared
to justify the losses incurred.[8] The limited utility of U.S.
global conventional military primacy has been evident in
wars against irregular adversaries, and it is no coincidence
that only such adversaries—in Vietnam, Lebanon, and Somalia—have imposed defeat or humiliation on the United
States.

The present counterinsurgent war the United States is
waging in Iraq has been compared to the Vietnam War. A
systematic assessment of the two conflicts reveals few
meaningful military analogies, but some political parallels,

including the challenge of maintaining domestic political support for presidential war policies in the middle of a protracted war, merit examination.[9] In Vietnam, years of escalating combat, mounting American casualties, and no convincing progress toward satisfaction of the policy objective of defeating the Communist threat to South Vietnam's survival slowly undermined public and congressional support for the war. Even before the watershed Tet Offensive in early 1968, public opinion was turning against the war. A Gallup poll taken in July 1967 revealed that 52 percent of Americans disapproved of the Johnson administration's handling of the war (only 34 percent approved). A month later another Gallup poll found, for the first time since the war began, that a majority of Americans (53 percent) believed that it had been a mistake to send U.S. troops to Vietnam.[10] By March 1969 a year after the Tet Offensive and four years after the deployment of U.S. ground combat forces to Vietnam, U.S. battle deaths equaled those of the highly unpopular Korean War, and nearly two out of three Americans polled said they would have opposed entry into the war had they known what it would cost in American lives.[11] It is little wonder that President Nixon, seeking to reduce U.S. casualty rates, began unilaterally withdrawing U.S. troops from Vietnam even though he clearly understood that a shrinking U.S. force presence reduced his bargaining leverage with the Communists.

U.S. casualties in Iraq have been low compared to those incurred in Vietnam. As of early January 2006, twenty-two hundred American military personnel had been killed in Iraq—only 3.7 percent of fifty-eight thousand American dead in Vietnam. The daily loss rate of slightly over two dead in Iraq is also much lower than the nineteen per day during the eight years of major U.S. combat operations in Vietnam.[12]

But the lower blood cost in Iraq does not necessarily guarantee continued public support for U.S. policy in that country. Though the strategic stakes in Iraq are arguably much greater than they ever were in Vietnam, prewar expectations of a quick and conclusive military victory and an easy transition to peace and stability did not materialize.

The Bush administration expected the Baathist regime, but not the Iraqi state itself, to collapse. The Iraqi state's unexpectedly abrupt and total administrative disintegration created a security vacuum throughout Iraq that coalition forces were unable to fill. An unanticipated insurgency emerged that continues to impede Iraq's physical and political reconstruction. Perhaps the most important influences on public support for the war were the intelligence failures that falsely convinced most Americans that Saddam Hussein's Iraq posed a growing WMD threat to the United States and repeated official declarations that Iraq and al Qaeda were allies.

It is of course impossible to predict the course of public attitudes toward the war in Iraq because the future course of the war itself is unknown. What is known is that public attitudes toward the decision to invade Iraq and the subsequent situation the United States encountered in Iraq have registered negative trends since the administration proclaimed the end of major U.S. combat operations on May 1, 2003. At the time, a Gallup poll revealed that 76 percent of Americans believed it was worth going to war, with only 19 percent contending that it was not. Since then, periodic Gallup polls have tracked a steady decline in public support, though the downward trend began to level off beginning in May 2004. Nevertheless, by mid-November 2005 only 40 percent of Americans polled said that it was worth going to war, while almost 60 percent said it was not. The same poll revealed that 59 percent believed the war in Iraq was going badly and only 40 percent believed it was going well. A mid-December poll revealed that 55 percent of Americans did not regard the war in Iraq as part of the war on terrorism, notwithstanding the Bush administration's insistence that Iraq was "the central front in the war on terrorism."

It is difficult, however, to read into these numbers any significant sentiment for withdrawing U.S. forces from Iraq and abandoning U.S. policy objectives there. Gallup polling from August 2003 through December 2005 revealed an average of only 25 percent of Americans favored abandoning Iraq.[13] President Bush's solid reelection in November 2004 to a second term on the issue of national security seemingly reinforced the conclusion of a major study on the relationship between casualties and public support that most Americans are "defeat phobic, not casualty phobic."[14]

By late 2005, however, there were signs of growing congressional and Republican unease over the course of events in Iraq. Continued insurgent attacks and U.S. casualties with no end in sight, and no apparent prospect of any significant near-term reduction below the baseline U.S. troop strength in Iraq of 138,000, combined to produce not only new polling lows on the war but also calls on Capitol Hill by Democrats and—for the first time—some Republicans for an exit strategy and date for U.S. withdrawal.

A third 1930s' strategic lesson for the United States today involves the risks inherent in discordance between foreign policy aims and military force posture. As we have seen, France's diplomatic strategy of enlisting continental allies to contain German expansionism was fatally undermined by an exclusively defensive military posture that left to Berlin the decision of when and under what circumstances a Franco–German war would occur. Indeed, even though France declared war on Germany in September 1939, the French army spent the next nine months sitting behind the Maginot line waiting for the Germans to attack. A force posture supportive of French diplomatic goals would have included a large standing mobile force capable of quickly attacking and overcoming German defenses in the Rhineland and moving on to threaten Germany's industrial heartland in the Ruhr. The French military instead chose a purely defensive posture and in so doing undermined the credibility of its defense guarantees to other states it attempted to enlist in the cause of containing German expansionism.

The fatal misfit between France's foreign and defense policies finds no analog with the United States today. The United States faces no equivalent of the German threat of the 1930s, and its activist foreign policy is properly supported by powerful and strategically mobile forces that can rapidly intervene virtually anywhere in the world. France in the 1930s renounced its great power status by denying itself offensive military capacity and by ceding to Britain the initiative in dealing with the Nazi threat. The contrast with the United States today could not be greater. In the first half decade of the twenty-first century the United States launched two wars: one in remote Afghanistan to overthrow the Taliban regime and disrupt al Qaeda's training base and a preventive war against Iraq to topple the regime of Saddam Hussein.

That said, however, there is a discernible and growing disjoint between the kind of war the United States prepares to fight and the kinds of wars it has actually fought. To put it another way, U.S. military force posture is increasingly at odds with the emerging strategic environment. The United States remains focused on preparation for high-technology conventional warfare against other potential military peer competitors (most notably China), whereas the predominant threats to its security interests are rogue states, failed states, and nonstate unconventional adversaries practicing asymmetrical war. This new threat environment places a premium on preparation for operations other than war (OOTW)[15]—that is, operations other than the big conventional force-on-force mission for which the U.S. military is optimized. Such operations include peace enforcement, counterinsurgency, stability, and state-building operations. Success in performing these operations is certainly essential to a foreign policy that embraces forcible regime change in places like Iraq and the muscular promotion of democracy in the Arab world and other regions of political autocracy and economic stagnation.

The limits of conventional military power in unconventional settings are as evident today in Iraq as they were in Vietnam forty years ago. Guerrilla warfare and terrorism are methods of violence selected by the militarily weak and applied against the conventional enemy's political will. Defeating adversaries practicing guerrilla warfare and terrorism requires both a dominant political strategy and the greatest discretion in the application of violence; it is necessary to defeat irregular adversaries politically as well as militarily, something the United States failed to do in Vietnam and may yet fail to do in Iraq.

Operation Iraqi Freedom (OIF) achieved a quick and complete victory over Iraq's conventional military forces, but that victory was not politically decisive because coalition forces did not seize full control of the country and impose the security necessary for Iraq's peaceful economic and political reconstruction. This failure was attributable in part to over a decade of U.S. ground force downsizing and the increasing substitution of technology for manpower, especially standoff precision air strikes for "boots on the ground." However, most OOTW, including counterinsurgency, are inherently manpower intensive and rely heavily on special skills—for example, human intelligence, civil affairs, police, public health, foreign language, foreign force training, and psychological warfare—that are secondary, even marginal, to the prosecution of conventional warfare. Forces capable of achieving swift conventional military victory may thus be quantitatively and qualitatively unsuited for postvictory tasks of the kind that the United States has encountered in Iraq. Strategic analyst Anthony H. Cordesman observes, with respect to OIF, that "a war is over only when violence is ended, military forces are no longer needed to provide security, and nation building can safely take place without military protection. It does not end with the defeat of the main enemy forces on the battlefield."[16] The Pentagon's loudly trumpeted focus on "transformation" of U.S. military forces remains fixated, however, on defeat of the enemy's main forces.

Military historian Antulio Echevarria believes the United States "is geared to fight wars as if they were battles and thus confuses the winning of campaigns or small-scale actions with the winning of wars." He further contends that "the characteristics of the U.S. style of warfare—speed, jointness, knowledge, and precision—are better suited for strike operations than for translating such operations into strategic successes."[17] British strategic analyst David J. Lonsdale concedes that America's strategic culture stresses "technological fixes to strategic problems" and "the increasing removal of humans from the sharp end of war," resulting in postmodern warfare "in which precise, distant bombardment dispenses with the need to deploy ground forces in a combat role and thereby relegates them to a constabulary function." He then warns that "these notions are not only astrategic and ignore the paradoxical logic of strategy; they also implicitly rely upon unrealistically effective operations, and thereby seemingly ignore the presence of friction."[18]

Military historian Frederick W. Kagan believes U.S. defense transformation itself is the primary culprit in delivering politically sterile military victories. The reason "the United States [has] been so successful in recent wars [but] encountered so much difficulty in securing its political aims after the shooting stopped," he argues, "lies partly in a 'vision of war' that see[s] the enemy as a target set and believe[s] that when all or most targets have been hit, he will inevitably surrender and American goals will be achieved." Unfortunately, this vision ignores the importance of "how, exactly, one defeats the enemy and what the enemy's country looks like at the moment the bullets stop flying." For Kagan, the "entire thrust of the current program of military transformation of the U.S. armed forces . . . aims at the implementation and perfection of this target set mentality."[19]

But target destruction is insufficient when the United States is seeking regime change in a manner that secures support of the defeated populace for the new government. Such circumstances require large numbers of properly trained troops for purposes of securing population centers and infrastructure, maintaining order, and providing humanitarian relief. Kagan continues,

> It is not enough to consider simply how to pound the enemy into submission with stand-off forces. . . . To effect regime change, U.S. forces must be positively in control of the enemy's territory and population as rapidly and continuously as possible. That control cannot be achieved by machines, still less by bombs. Only humans beings interacting with human beings can achieve it. The only hope for success in the extension of politics that is war is to restore the human element to the transformation equation.[20]

It appears that in Iraq the Pentagon simply lost sight of the main U.S. political objective, which was not the destruction of Iraqi military forces but rather effecting Iraq's successful reconstruction. To be sure, the former was a precondition for the latter, but the latter was an especially, perhaps impossibly, tall order for a military "obsessed with stupendous deeds of fire and movement rather than the political functions that war must serve."[21] Strategic analyst Colin Gray contends that though "the transformation push may well succeed and be highly impressive in its military-technical accomplishments, it is likely to miss the most vital marks." Why?

> There are a number of reasons for this harsh judgment. First, high-tech transformation will have only modest value, because war is a duel and all of America's foes out to 2020 will be significantly asymmetrical. The most intelligent among them, as well as the geographically more fortunate and the luckier, will pursue ways of war that do not test U.S. strengths. Second, the military potential of this transformation, as with all past transformations, is being undercut by the unstoppable processes of diffusion which spread technology and ideas. Third, the transformation that is being sought appears to be oblivious to the fact . . . that there is more to war than warfare. War is about the peace it will shape. It is not obvious that the current process of military transformation will prove vitally useful in helping to improve America's strategic performance. Specifically, the country needs to approach the waging of war as political behavior for political purposes. Sometimes one is moved to the despairing conclusion that Clausewitz wrote in vain, for all the influence he has had on the American way of war.[22]

None of the foregoing is to argue against continued conventional military perfection. U.S. conventional military primacy is inherently desirable because it deters an enemy attack in kind and effectively eliminates conventional warfare as a means of settling disputes with the United States—no mean accomplishments. Conventional primacy also permits the United States to easily crush the conventionally weak and incompetent, like the Taliban in Afghanistan and the Baathist government in Iraq. Conventional primacy, at least of the kind sought by the "transformationists" in the Pentagon, also permits increasing substitution of machines for manpower—more specifically, standoff air strikes for close ground combat—which in turn has reduced U.S. casualty rates to historic lows and has arguably increased public tolerance for the use of force overseas. "Although conventional conflict may look unlikely now, the United States must maintain its ability to fight major states—something the British Army failed to do, thereby inviting German aggression in 1914 and 1939," argues Max Boot. But he also cautions the Pentagon to "recall what happened the last time it failed to take guerrilla warfare seriously; that time was the 1960s, and the United States was just starting to get embroiled in a conflict in Vietnam."[23]

The same primacy that has produced conventional deterrence has pushed America's enemies into greater reliance on irregular warfare responses that expose the limits of conventional primacy.[24] Even in the case of war with China it is most unlikely that the Chinese would be foolish enough to pit their conventional weaknesses against U.S. conventional strengths (e.g., airpower). During the Korean War, the People's Liberation Army pitted its strengths—manpower superiority, night operations, infiltration tactics, logistical austerity, and off-road mobility—against round-bound, firepower-dependent U.S. forces and managed to stalemate the conflict for two years. Robert Kaplan believes the Chinese will again "approach us asymmetrically, as terrorists do. In Iraq the insurgents have shown us the low end of asymmetry, with car bombs. But the Chinese are poised to show us the high end of the art. That is the threat."[25] He expects the Chinese will pit cruise missiles and quiet diesel submarines against U.S. aircraft carriers and other surface warships. The Chinese could also launch hundreds of cruise and ballistic missiles against Taiwan before U.S. forces could get to the island to defend it. Nor could any prudent war planner rule out Beijing-sponsored terrorist attacks on the American homeland. There is also the question of how the United States could or would terminate a war with an enemy that is more or less immune to invasion. Even in the case of Iraq, which the United States did invade and occupy in 2003, decisive war termination remains elusive.

With respect to the experience of the Iraq War and the established relationship between terrorism and weak and failed states, the policy issue is not whether the United States should continue to perfect its conventional primacy, but whether, given the evolving strategic environment of deconventionalized combat, it should create ground (and supporting air) forces dedicated to performing operations other than war, including counterinsurgency, peace enforcement, and state building.[26] Extant conventional ground force and operational/tactical doctrines are not suitable for counterinsurgency, peace enforcement, and other OOTW. The starting point of rules of engagement for such operations is the imperative of utmost restraint and discrimination in the application of force. Firepower is the instrument of last rather than first resort. There is no big enemy to close with and destroy, but rather the presence of threatened civilian populations, which must be protected in ways that minimize collateral damage. Conventional ground force preparation for OOTW accordingly requires major doctrinal and training deprogramming of conventional military habits and reprogramming with the alien tactics, doctrines, and heavy political oversight of OOTW. Needless to say, forces so reprogrammed—commonly manpower-intensive and relatively low firepower—will not be optimized for big, high-technology conventional conflicts.

Unfortunately, whatever the strength of the arguments for establishment of OOTW-dedicated ground forces (and there are serious arguments against), such forces stand little bureaucratic chance of ever seeing the light of day. The Pentagon prepares for the kind of wars it wants to fight— that is, wars it is good at fighting—rather than the wars it may actually fight—that is, wars it is not so good at fighting. Marine Corps colonel Thomas X. Hammes observes that though unconventional war "is the only kind of war America has ever lost," the Defense Department (DOD) "has largely ignored unconventional warfare." He adds, "As the only Goliath left in the world, we should be worried that the world's Davids have found a sling and a stone that work. Yet internal DOD debate has largely ignored this striking difference between the outcomes of conventional and unconventional warfare."[27] Steven Metz and Raymond Millen observe that though "the strategic salience of insurgency for the United States is higher than it has been since the height of the Cold War," insurgency "remains challenging for the United States because two of its dominant characteristics—protractedness and ambiguity—mitigate the effectiveness of the American military."[28]

Institutional resistance is especially strong inside the U.S. Army, notwithstanding recent growth in its special operations force components. Though the Marine Corps is comfortable with counterinsurgency because of its long history of imperial policing operations (in 1990 it reissued its classic 1940 *Small Wars Manual*), the army has never viewed counterinsurgency as anything other than a diversion from its main mission: conventional combat against like enemies. The experience of the Vietnam War reinforced the army's aversion to counterinsurgency, which the army ignored in terms of training and doctrine until it again encountered the Iraq insurgency.[29] It studiously avoided "lessons learned" drills because such drills would have implied a necessity to prepare for more insurgent challenges.[30] "Iraq underscores . . . the overwhelming organizational tendency within the U.S. military not to absorb historical lessons when planning and conducting counterinsurgency operations," concludes a 2005 Rand Corporation study delivered to Secretary of Defense Donald Rumsfeld. The study proceeded to recommend that

In the future, U.S. military forces engaged in counterinsurgency operations must be composed of personnel with training and skills similar to special operations forces, i.e., the language and culture of the country, and in the critically important political, economic, intelligence, organizational, and psychological dimensions of counterinsurgency warfare. Serious attention should also be given to creating in the Army a dedicated cadre of counterinsurgency specialists and a program to produce such experts.[31]

None of this is to argue that the Defense Department is hopelessly unadaptable to the deconventionalized global strategic environment—only that its force structural bias toward conventional combat is long standing and well entrenched and that overcoming that bias will entail fundamental changes in how U.S. military forces are organized, equipped, trained, and manned. For example, personnel policies that constantly rotate individuals from one assignment to another and promotion polices prejudiced against development of specialized area knowledge and linguistic skills are antithetical to the requirements of successful counterinsurgency. For another example, retention of division-level organizations makes little sense against decentralized, irregular adversaries. And what does the F/A-22 program bring to the table in the fight against al Qaeda?

There is, encouragingly, some evidence that the 9/11 attacks and subsequent experience in Afghanistan and Iraq are sparking a shift in the Pentagon's future focus in the direction of counterinsurgency and counterterrorism, homeland defense against terrorist attacks, and operations aimed at preventing rogue state and terrorist organization acquisition of weapons of mass destruction. (OIF arguably was the first war waged to prevent a hostile state from acquiring nuclear weapons.) These are some of the taskings of the February 2006 *Quadrennial Defense Review* (*QDR*).[32] A new and refocused *QDR* does not, however, constitute an adequate test of the seriousness of the Pentagon's commitment to change; talk is cheap. The real test will be in translating the rhetorical mandates of the *QDR* into rewritten doctrine and altered procurement, organizational, and manpower policies.

The dangers of strategic overextension constitute the fourth pertinent lesson of the 1930s. Not only is there a misfit between the kind of war the Pentagon is prepared to fight and the kinds of wars it is now fighting and has been fighting since the end of the cold war, there is also evidence that the United States is on the verge of potentially dangerous strategic overextension. To be sure, no great power maintains standing military forces to cover all of its strategic bets simultaneously. The issue is not the disparity between means and ends, but rather the point at which the scope of that disparity becomes an unacceptable strategic risk.

During the 1930s Britain suffered a huge and unbridgeable gap between its supply of military power and potential military power and the demands on that power. Threatened in Europe by Nazi Germany, in the Mediterranean by Fascist Italy, and in the Far East by Imperial Japan, Britain survived World War II only by virtue of Hitler's fatal decisions to invade the Soviet Union and declare war on the United States. Strategically, Britain faced about as awful a worst-case scenario as any great power has in modern times, and the failure of its appeasement policy in Europe and East Asia rendered the enlistment of powerful allies Britain's only salvation.

The degree of Britain's strategic overextension in the 1930s has no analogy to the United States today, though the potential for unacceptable strategic risk has emerged since the U.S. invasion in Iraq and especially with respect to ground forces. Between the first and second U.S. wars with Iraq, the George H. W. Bush and Clinton administrations reduced the size of active-duty U.S. military forces by about 40 percent, but in the second war against Iraq the Pentagon incurred unexpected and continuing demands on its ground forces and so far has chosen not to increase their permanently authorized strength. The result has been a highly stressed all-volunteer army and the commitment of about 90 percent of U.S. ground forces (deployed army and Marine Corps forces plus their rotation bases) to counterterrorist operations in Afghanistan and counterinsurgency operations in Iraq, leaving little else available for contingencies that may arise elsewhere—the Korean peninsula, for example.[33] Whether this is a prudent strategic risk is a matter of judgment. Suffice it to say, present U.S. ground force deployments in Iraq and Afghanistan more or less preclude Iraq-style regime-change operations (though not air and missile strikes) against other rogue states. This point was conceded in early 2005 by the chairman of the Joint Chiefs of Staff, Gen. Richard Myers, and this may explain in part why the United States is pursuing diplomatic solutions to perceived nuclear proliferation threats by North Korea and Iran.[34] As Richard Haass, who served in the first George W. Bush administration as director of the State Department's Policy Planning Staff, points out,

> the fact remains that quality cannot always substitute fully for quantity. Some tasks (in particular those that do not involve combat on open battlefields such as post-conflict stability operations) require a great deal of manpower. The result is that the United States would be hard pressed to respond to a full-fledged crisis on the Korean Peninsula without reducing its commitment to Iraq—or to try to replicate anywhere else what it is doing in Iraq or to intervene on a large scale in some humanitarian crisis such as in Darfur.[35]

The war in Iraq has greatly weakened U.S. capacity to meet the Defense Department's post–cold war force planning standard of being able to wage two nearly simultaneous major regional wars.

If the size of U.S. ground forces has become an issue, so too has their composition. Of the combined total active-duty end-strength of the army and Marine Corps of 677,000, only 71,000, or slightly over 10 percent, are infantry.[36] Yet infantry forms the core of military operations against irregular adversaries. Boot believes that the emerging strategic environment will be dominated by irregular warfare threats and that this mandates adding "at least 100,000 soldiers, and probably a good deal more" to the active-duty U.S. military, and he would finance that increase by reducing or canceling such big-ticket procurement programs as the F/A-22 fighter, national missile defense, and the Virginia-class submarine.[37] Military manpower expert Lawrence Korb has called for adding at least eighty-six thousand soldiers to the army in the form of two specially trained "peacekeeping and stabilization divisions."[38] Retired general Barry McCaffrey, who led the army's Twenty-fourth Infantry Division in the Gulf War of 1991, believes the army needs to increase by eighty thousand personnel and the Marine Corps by twenty-five thousand.[39]

The Defense Department is in a quandary. It is committed to an expensive transformation of U.S. military forces in a manner that accelerates substitution of advanced technology for manpower. At the same time, it is not only waging an expensive, manpower-intensive counterinsurgent war in Iraq but also entering a new strategic environment in which the threat spectrum is dominated by irregular and other forms of asymmetrical warfare. The department is already seeking to transfer dollars from planned big-ticket navy and air force procurement programs to an army severely stressed by operations in Iraq,[40] but the department does not believe that a larger army is necessary.[41] Therefore, any significant increase in the authorized end-strength of U.S. ground forces, barring an unlikely big defense budget boost, would have to be taken out of the hide of defense transformation. The trade-off is essentially between the counterinsurgent war at hand in Iraq versus preparation for future conventional war.[42]

Critics contend that the Defense Department's opposition to both increased U.S. forces in Iraq and permanent increases in authorized army and Marine Corps end-strengths has not only hampered the U.S. counterinsurgency effort in Iraq but also strained the all-volunteer army, including its reserve components, to the breaking point. Protraction of an unexpected insurgency in Iraq has compelled repeated and extended tours of combat duty for both active-duty and reserve forces; this has adversely affected army recruiting to the point where the active-duty army has lowered entrance standards, cut minimum enlistment to fifteen months, and doubled its signing bonus to $40,000. The Army National Guard and Army Reserve, which account for 40 percent of all army personnel in Iraq, have been compelled to raise their maximum age for recruits from thirty-four years old to thirty-nine.[43] Notwithstanding these measures, however, shortfalls in army recruiting continue to rise, prompting several observers, including Charles Moskos, the dean of America's military sociologists, to call for a return of the draft. Other observers point to the potential implications of insufficient volunteers for the image of America's will in the war on terrorism.[44] As a former Pentagon public affairs official put it, "Consider the implications of being unable to find sufficient volunteers, as seen by our adversaries. Has the United States lost its will to survive? What's happened to the Great Satan when so few are willing to fight to defend the country? Surely bin Laden, et al. are making this argument, telling supporters victory is just around the corner if they are a bit more patient."[45]

In 1939 Britain reinstituted conscription because it could no longer cover potential demands on its military power in Europe, the Mediterranean, and the Far East through reliance on volunteers. For the United States in the first decade of the twenty-first century, however, conscription is not a politically viable option—the administration, Congress, and the American public oppose a return to the draft—notwithstanding the military manpower recruiting and retention crisis occasioned by a protracted war in Iraq and Defense Department opposition to a larger army.

We have so far focused on one of two ways of solving the problem of strategic overextension: boosting means. The other is to reduce ends. Realist and other critics of post-9/11 U.S. foreign policy, the tenets of which are enshrined in President George W. Bush's September 2002 *National Security Strategy of the United States of America*, contend that the United States has embraced a set of exceptionally ambitious foreign policy objectives that are inherently unobtainable, politically unsustainable, or both. In place of an interest-based foreign policy (which characterized the George H. W. Bush administration), the George W. Bush administration has substituted a values-based, neoconservative ideology-driven foreign policy that has alienated allies, emboldened adversaries, and led the United States into an unnecessary and enervating war in Iraq.

In the latter half of 2003, at the request of the U.S. Army's Strategic Studies Institute, I undertook an assessment of the objectives of the global war on terrorism as defined by the administration. The study, *Bounding the Global War on Terrorism*,[46] examined scores of major official documents and pronouncements and discovered no fewer than six objectives: (1) destroy the perpetrators of the 9/11 attacks—that is, al Qaeda; (2) destroy or defeat other terrorist organizations of global reach, including their regional and national affiliates; (3) delegitimize and ultimately eradicate the phenomenon of terrorism itself; (4) transform Iraq into a prosperous, stable democracy; (5) transform the Middle East into a region of participatory self-government and economic opportunity, using the new Iraq as a political beacon; and (6) halt, by force if necessary, the continued proliferation of weapons of mass destruction and their means of delivery to hostile and potentially hostile states and other entities. The study also judged that conflating al Qaeda and Saddam Hussein's Iraq, and more generally rogue states and terrorist organizations, as a monolithic threat was a strategic error of the first order because it ignored key differences in their nature, interests, and vulnerability to credible nuclear and conventional deterrence.[47] Conflation also implied that Iraq was complicit in the 9/11 attack, an implication that clearly served the case for war against Iraq but one that remains unsupported by any evidence.

The study argued that the Iraq War, far from being an integral component of the war on terrorism was actually an enervating detour from it—indeed, the U.S. invasion and occupation of Iraq risked transforming that country into a recruiting and training ground for al Qaeda and other radical Islamic groups. This conclusion was supported by subsequent events and studies. Suicide terrorism expert Robert Pape noted in his seminal 2005 book, *Dying to Win: The Strategic Logic of Suicide Terrorism*, that, prior to the U.S. overthrow of Saddam Hussein, Iraq had never experienced even a single suicide attack and warned that "the close association between foreign military occupations and the growth of suicide terrorist movements in the occupied regions should make us hesitate over any strategy centering on the transformation of Muslim societies by means of . . . military power."[48] A classified CIA assessment leaked in the same year concluded that Iraq was becoming "an even more effective training ground for Islamic extremists than Afghanistan was in al Qaeda's early days" and that as such the war in Iraq was "likely to produce a dangerous legacy by dispersing to other countries Iraqi and foreign combatants more adept and better organized than they were before the conflict."[49] Middle East terrorism experts Daniel Benjamin and Steven Simon, in their 2005 book, *The Next Attack: The Failure of the War on Terrorism and a Strategy for Getting It Right*, write that Osama bin Laden was the chief beneficiary of the U.S. invasion of Iraq.

> The terrorists have found in Iraq a better sanctuary, training ground, and laboratory than they ever had in Afghanistan. They have also been given what they desire most: American targets in close proximity. They can now demonstrate their valor and resolve to bleed America, and in doing so, to build momentum for their cause. We have slain the chimera of Saddam Hussein's Iraq, but we are nourishing the all-too-real dragon of radical Islam.
>
> It is unlikely that even in his most feverish reveries, Usama bin Laden could have imagined that America would stumble so badly and wound itself so grievously. By occupying Iraq, the United States has played into the hands of its opponents, affirming the story they have been telling to the Muslim world and adding to their aura as true warriors in defense of Islam.[50]

Having identified the stated objectives of the war on terrorism, *Bounding the Global War on Terrorism* then proceeded to assess the feasibility of each objective. It concluded that destroying al Qaeda, or at least reducing it to a significantly lesser threat, and transforming Iraq into some kind of democracy were not inherently unrealistic goals, although al Qaeda is much more than an organization (it is also an inspirational symbol of Islamic radicalism) and critical U.S. mistakes in post-Baathist Iraq cast serious doubt over prospects for both stability and democracy in that country—and by extension the political transformation of the Middle East.[51] Even absent those mistakes the challenges would have entailed exceptional risks. As a subsequent Strategic Studies Institute assessment by Stephen Biddle observed,

> Political engineering on this scale could easily go awry. It is far from clear whether stable democracy can be built from the ruins of a Ba'athist police state in Iraq, even with all the money and soldiers we can provide. And if democratization fails, the result could be dangerous instability. Historically, the most war-prone states are not autocracies—they are regimes in the early stages of transition from autocracy to democracy. To multiply the opportunities for such unstable transitions across the region is to create a serious risk of major war.[52]

My study further concluded that the goal of destroying all international terrorist organizations and their local affiliates, to say nothing of eradicating terrorism as a method of violence, was inherently unrealistic and also dangerous because it pitted the United States against "enemies" that had not threatened it. Again, the Biddle assessment:

> In a world where the interconnections among terrorist groups are ambiguous, a central aim of American strategy ought . . . to be to drive wedges between these groups wherever possible—to *reduce*, not increase, their marginal proclivity for cooperation and joint action against us. A broad but unspecific definition of the enemy that refuses to exclude any meaningful terrorist group could easily do just the opposite, unifying a polyglot terrorist alliance, and risking self-fulfilling prophecy by driving together groups that would otherwise have sat on the sidelines rather than making war on distant America.[53]

Zbigniew Brzezinski has also remarked on the muddiness of the threat definition.

The difficulty is that the administration's definition of what and whom Americans are being asked to fight in "the war on terrorism" has been articulated in a remarkably vague fashion. Matters have not been made clear by the president's reduction (or elevation, depending on one's vantage point) of terrorists to "evildoers," otherwise unidentified, whose motivations are said to be simply satanic. Identifying terrorism itself as the enemy also blithely ignored the fact that terrorism is a lethal technique for intimidation. . . . One does not wage a war against a technique or a tactic.[54]

Clarity of threat definition was hardly improved by the Defense Department's failed attempt in the summer of 2005 to drop the term "global war on terrorism" in its rhetoric in favor of "global struggle against violent extremism." According to Gen. Richard B. Meyers, then-chairman of the Joint Chiefs of Staff, the use of the term "war" implied there was a military solution to the problem; "struggle" was more appropriate because the solution was "more political, more economic than it is military." As for the term "terrorism," it was simply the "method [violent extremists] use." Meyers was not clear on what "violent extremism" included and excluded in terms of targets requiring U.S. military and nonmilitary action.[55]

Presenting terrorism and terrorists (or "violent extremists") as simply manifestations of evil denies them any political context and in so doing reduces the war on terrorism to a manhunt. To be sure, terrorists must be hunted down, but terrorist organizations are in the business of terrorism because they believe it advances political objectives—for example, the liberation of the West Bank from Israeli occupation, the expulsion of the United States from the Middle East, the toppling of pro-Western Arab regimes. Terrorism, like war, is an extension of politics by other means. Al Qaeda attacked the United States on 9/11 not because of "who we are" (all secular states, including Muslim ones, are anathema to Osama bin Laden) but rather because of "what we do"—that is, the U.S. policies of maintaining a military presence in the Persian Gulf, backing "apostate" Arab governments, and supporting Israel. "Muslims do not 'hate our freedom,' but rather, they hate our policies," concluded a September 2004 study by the Pentagon's Defense Science Board. "The overwhelming majority voice their objections to what they see as one-sided support in favor of Israel and against Palestinian rights, and the long-standing, even increasing support for what Muslims collectively see as tyrannies, most notably Egypt, Saudi Arabia, Jordan, Pakistan, and the Gulf states."[56] In this regard, the U.S. invasion of Iraq in 2003 offered bin Laden a strategic opportunity. Not only did the invasion remove a thoroughly secular (and therefore "apostate") regime; in addition, in the judgment of the highly respected London-based International Institute for Strategic Studies, the

> U.S.-led invasion and occupation of Iraq intensified many Muslims' worries about America's global intentions and made them more easily seduced by Osama bin Laden's arguments. He was able to cast the war quite persuasively as confirmation of Washington's wish to dominate the Arab and larger Muslim world politically, economically and militarily; its intention to loot Islam of its natural resources, in particular oil; and its inexorable support for Israel's repression of Palestinian Muslims. This rhetorical power seemed only to have reinforced the al-Qaeda leadership's extreme and non-negotiable agenda, which calls for the debilitation of the United States as a superpower through apocalypse, the overthrow of "apostate" Arab regimes and the establishment of a global Islamic caliphate.[57]

Fawaz A. Gerges, in his exceptionally insightful *The Far Enemy: Why Jihad Went Global*, contends that the Iraq War revived al Qaeda's flagging fortunes.

> In the case of bin Laden, Iraq has become an open front in the global war against the United States and its allies, and Zarqawi, who leads the jihadist

contingency there, has offered him leadership on a
silver platter. The global war is not going well for
bin Laden, and Iraq presented him, as he said, with
a 'golden and unique opportunity' to expand the confrontation against the United States and convince
his jihadist cohorts and Muslims worldwide that al
Qaeda is still alive despite crippling operational set-
backs in Afghanistan, Pakistan, Saudi Arabia, Yemen,
and elsewhere.[58]

Bzrezinski rightly cautions that the "American reluctance to recognize a connection between the events of 9/11
and the modern political history of the Middle East—with
its strong political passions, nurtured by religious fanati-
cism and zealous nationalism, unstably coexisting with political weakness—is a dangerous form of denial."[59]
With respect to preventing determined and resource-
ful rogue states from acquiring weapons of mass destruction, especially nuclear weapons, *Bounding the Global War
of Terrorism* concludes that the goal might be achievable
but only at the risk of dangerous military action and even
war. The study notes that the U.S. preventive war against
Iraq, which was justified by the perceived imperative of stopping Saddam Hussein from acquiring nuclear weapons, had
no apparent deterrent effect on North Korea or Iran, which
accelerated their nuclear weapons programs precisely to
avoid the Baathist regime's fate.
The study's summary judgment is that "the global war
on terrorism as currently defined and waged is dangerously
indiscriminate and ambitious, and [therefore] that its parameters should be readjusted to conform to concrete U.S.
security interests and the limits of American power."[60] A
realistically bounded global war on terrorism, the study
contended, mandated (1) deconflation of the terrorist/rogue
state threat; (2) substitution of credible deterrence for preventive war as the primary policy for dealing with rogue
states seeking to acquire nuclear weapons; (3) reorienta-
tion of the war on terrorism first and foremost on al Qaeda,
its allies, and homeland security; (4) pursuit of rogue-state
regime change via measures short of war; and (5) readiness

to settle for stability rather than democracy in Iraq and international rather than U.S. responsibility for Iraq.

To the vaulting objectives of the war on terrorism and their unexpected risks and resource costs in post-Baathist Iraq must be added the Bush adminstration's remarkable objective of maintaining military forces "strong enough to dissuade potential adversaries from pursuing a military build-up in hopes of surpassing, or equaling, the power of the United States." With respect to perpetual American global military supremacy, China is enjoined to desist from "pursuing advanced military capabilities that can threaten its neighbors in the Asia–Pacific region" and warned not to continue "following [that] outdated path [to] national greatness."[61]

The limits of U.S. conventional military power have been discussed. To the thesis of global conventional military dominance, America's adversaries have responded with the antithesis of asymmetric warfare both below and above the conventional threshold. Intelligent enemies are not going to try to beat us at our own game, and China is hardly going to cow before the arrogance of being lectured not to pursue the very path of military strength the United States has chosen. On the contrary, China will continue to spend a considerable portion of its exploding wealth on modernizing its armed forces for possible war with a United States whose continued military domination of offshore East Asia is not acceptable, and China will modernize in a fashion that will compromise full U.S. exploitation of conventional superiority in naval power and airpower.[62] It is as absurd to believe that any great power can immunize itself from inevitable relative decline as it is to believe that China, with its long history as the Middle Kingdom and its irresistible determination to erase two centuries of humiliation at the hands of the West, can be dissuaded from acquiring military power commensurate its wealth and ambitions. What is the United States prepared to do if China is not dissuaded? Launch a preventive war? Shut down Wal-Mart as a source of China's burgeoning foreign exchange reserves? Prohibit China from financing U.S. deficit spending? There is certainly nothing to be gained by publicly declaring China an enemy and condemning its domestic political system. Robert Merry contends that

> The economic and military rise of China in East Asia is inevitable. The only question is whether America can find a way to accommodate this emerging reality while retaining the measure of regional influence and avoiding war with a landmass nation with 1.2 billion people and millions more ethnic brethren throughout Asia. This is going to require deft diplomacy, an appreciation for the cultural underpinnings of the Sinic civilization, and strong alliances with Russia, Japan, India, and any other nation that serves as a counterweight to China. A policy of verbal or economic bellicosity in response to China's expansion of influence and power . . . is precisely the worst course that America could adopt at a time when it is struggling with Islamic terrorism.[63]

One hopes that experience in post-Baathist Iraq has educated the United States on the potential risks and costs of preventive war. The elevation of preventive war as the centerpiece of declared U.S. national security strategy and its selection as a means of counterproliferation has not only saddled the United States with a costly and open-ended irregular war but also alienated much of the international community, including key European allies, which had provided broad support for U.S. military action in Afghanistan. Preventive war exacerbates America's strategic overstretch because it unnecessarily devours U.S. military resources while simultaneously depriving the United States of potential support. Most of the international community approved of U.S. military action to attack al Qaeda and the Taliban regime in Afghanistan because that action was a legitimate exercise in self-defense in the wake of the 9/11 attacks on the United States; it disapproved of the U.S. invasion of Iraq because the attack violated the central norm of post-1945 international political system and could not be justified as legitimate self-defense.

A fifth lesson of the 1930s for the United States today is the importance of maintaining a proper offensive-defensive balance. We have seen in the case of France in the interwar period an insistence on a purely defensive military strategy that undermined French diplomacy and ceded the initiative for war to Nazi Germany. However, the French General Staff and most other professional military observers in Europe, including German military leaders, assumed that in the event of war France, supported by Britain, could effectively deny Germany a swift and decisive victory, thereby forcing Germany into a long war of attrition in which superior Anglo–French (and hopefully American) resources would prevail over time. Indeed, but for Hitler's personal intervention of behalf of a daring plan of attack proposed by Gen. Erich von Manstein as a substitute for the General Staff's unimaginative war plan, the French probably would have denied Germany the crushing victory of 1940.[64]

In contrast to France in the interwar period, the United States since the outbreak of World War II has fought all of its wars overseas. Having little need to pay attention to its own territorial defense (the War of 1812 occasioned the last foreign invasion of the United States)[65] but embracing an activist foreign policy dedicated to preserving order and stability, the United States has created military forces capable of worldwide intervention. And these forces have proved their utility in both the post–cold war and the post-9/11 eras: they quickly overthrew the Taliban regime in Afghanistan and the Saddam Hussein regime in Iraq.

The question of the proper offensive-defensive balance has nonetheless arisen with respect to America's self-declared war on terrorism, which engages a variety of government agencies and resources other than the Department of Defense, most notably the new Department of Homeland Security, a bureaucratic consolidation of almost two dozen federal agencies and two hundred thousand employees. That war is being prosecuted with a necessarily predominant focus on the offense—disrupting and destroying terrorist threats before they materialize in attacks on the United States and U.S. interests overseas. No one disputes the need to "take the war to the terrorists" or the difficulty of winning wars on the defensive, though a good defense, as the 1940 Battle of Britain demonstrated, can save a country from losing a war. But a neglected defense is a standing invitation to enemy attack, and there is no reason to believe offensive operations against al Qaeda have rendered the organization incapable of scoring another 9/11. (And if the 2004 Madrid and 2005 London mass transit bombings are any indication, the next attackers are probably already resident in the United States and Europe.)

The argument that the war in Iraq serves as a magnet for terrorists that otherwise would be conducting attacks in the United States is not persuasive. The war certainly did not prevent the Madrid and London attacks. Iraqis are notable for their scarcity among the ranks of Islamic terrorists, and 90 to 95 percent of insurgents in Iraq are Iraqis radicalized by the dispossession of the Baathist regime and/ or the U.S. invasion and occupation of their country. True, most suicide bombings in Iraq have been conducted by outsiders—mostly Saudis, Syrians, and Kuwaitis—but studies of suicide bombers in Iraq by the Saudi government and an Israeli think tank reveal that the great majority of them had never taken part in any terrorist activity before their arrival in Iraq but rather were radicalized by the Iraq War itself.[66] They are part of a new generation of terrorists responding to calls by Osama bin Laden and radical Islamic clerics to defend their fellow Muslims from the "infidel crusaders" in Iraq. Notes terrorism expert Peter Bergen, "The president is right that Iraq is a main front in the war on terrorism, but this is a front we created."[67]

The policy issue is whether the offensive side of the war on terrorism is diverting too much attention and resources away from the defensive side. All strategic choices involve opportunity costs. Dollars spent on suppressing the Iraqi insurgency and reconstructing Iraq are dollars that could be spent on such homeland security tasks as improving the security of America's critical energy, food, chemical, transportation, and financial infrastructure.

Stephen Flynn noted in late 2004 that the federal government "spends more every three days to finance the war in Iraq than it has provided over the past three years to prop up the security of all 361 U.S. commercial seaports." He went on to deplore "a myopic focus on conventional military forces at the expense of domestic security," citing the fact that the fiscal year 2005 federal budget allocated $7.6 billion to improve security of U.S. military bases in the United States but only $2.6 billion to protect "all the vital systems throughout the country that sustain a modern society."[68] A 2003 Council on Foreign Relations study concluded that "the United States remains dangerously ill prepared to handle a catastrophic attack on American soil" because of, among other things, "acute shortages of radios among firefighters, WMD protective gear for police departments, basic equipment and expertise in public health laboratories, and hazardous materials detection equipment in most cities."[69] A special assessment of aviation security prepared by the FBI and the Department of Homeland Security in 2005 concluded that despite a huge post-9/11 investment in security the aviation system remains vulnerable to terrorist attack, especially with respect to chartered planes, cargo aircraft, general aviation, and helicopters, all of which are less well guarded than commercial airliners.[70] A *New York Times* assessment notes the presence in the United States of 123 chemical plants, each of which could, in a worst-case terrorist attack, endanger a million people or more.[71] The Environmental Protection Agency lists 823 sites where the casualty toll from a catastrophic disaster at a chemical plant could run from one hundred thousand to over a million people; yet no federal law establishes minimum security standards at chemical facilities.[72] Some facilities have little more than chain-link fences surrounding them, a reflection of the inherent private sector antagonism between security costs and profit margins.[73]

In December 2005—more than four years after the 9/11 attacks—the 9/11 Commission issued its final report. The report graded post-9/11 U.S. performance in a variety of areas, including homeland security and emergency preparedness and response. It was not a report card any grammar school student would wish to show his parents. The commission assigned Fs in three areas: provision of adequate radio spectrum for first responders, allocation of homeland security funds based on risk, and improvement in airline passenger prescreening. It awarded Ds in the areas of critical infrastructure risks and vulnerabilities assessment, checked luggage and cargo screening, and international collaboration on borders and document security. The rest of the grades consisted of five Cs and two Bs; there were no As.[74]

Graham Allison, in his assessment of U.S. vulnerability to nuclear terrorism, says that the United States has "no coherent strategy for combating nuclear terrorism" and that "Americans are no safer from a nuclear terrorist attack today than we were on September 10, 2001."[75] He notes, among many other things, that none of the 103 operating nuclear reactors in the United States, twenty-one of them located within five miles of an airport, was designed to withstand the impact of a Boeing 767 jetliner.[76]

The above is but a small sample of the litany of assessed homeland vulnerabilities to terrorist attacks that appear almost daily in the press, especially the broadcast media. It is a litany that suggests that the United States still does not have its homeland security act together and thus is not winning the defensive side of the war on terrorism. It further suggests that the principal opportunity cost of prolonged counterinsurgent warfare may well be lost investment in homeland security. Benjamin and Simon contend that

> With defense relegated to the back burner, there has been little presidential or congressional oversight, weak departmental leadership, inadequate coordination between Washington and state and local governments, poor collaboration with the private sector, and only half-hearted attempts to reform entrenched interests, like the FBI, that had strong constituencies on Capitol Hill. Most regrettably, there was no perceived need for a strategy that would balance risk and resources to produce priorities for homeland defense, nor was there a vision of the endstate—of a secure America—and therefore no sense of how much would be effort enough to ensure that we could weather an attack without stalling economically, unraveling as a society, or failing to destroy our assailant.[77]

The disastrously belated and disjointed responses of federal, state, and local agencies to Hurricane Katrina vindicated this assessment; especially disturbing was the manifest incompetence of the Federal Emergency Management Agency.

A final 1930s lesson is the virtue of consistency in threatening and using force. World War II began when Hitler miscalculated Anglo–French willingness to fight for Poland. He assumed, not unreasonably, that London and Paris would stand aside as he gobbled up Poland; after all, they had done nothing when he reoccupied the Rhineland, nothing when he absorbed Austria, and nothing but capitulate to his demand for the Sudetenland. Why would they fight for Poland when they chose not to fight for Czechoslovakia? Appeasement had established a pattern that predicted Anglo–French inaction over Poland. Viewed from the German side, a policy of threatening war had established a pattern that predicted further easy success for Nazi territorial expansion. Hitler was going to have a free hand in eastern Europe within the parameters of the deal he had cut with Stalin (Hitler would finish off Stalin later), and the British and French were not going to do anything about it. Thus the Anglo–French decision to declare war came as a rude surprise.

When it comes to threatening and using force, unpredictability can keep adversaries guessing, but it can also encourage adversaries to launch wars in the mistaken belief that they can get away with them. The North Korean invasion of South Korea in 1950 and the Iraqi invasion of Kuwait forty years later were launched on the wrong assumption that the United States would not respond militarily. In the former case, it was reasonable for Stalin and Kim Il-sung to conclude that the United States would not fight to defend South Korea. The United States had refused to intervene militarily on behalf of the nationalist government in China (if it would not fight to save China from Communism, why would it fight for such a comparatively unimportant country as South Korea?); it had withdrawn its occupation forces from South Korea; and it had publicly declared that South Korea lay beyond America's defense perimeter.[78] In the case of Iraqi aggression in 1990, Saddam Hussein, with whom the United States had served as a de facto cobelligerent in Iraq's war with Iran, reasonably concluded that he could get away with the invasion of a country that enjoyed no defense relationship with United States, especially after the State Department declared that the United States did not take sides in Arab territorial disputes.[79]

A key element in Saddam Hussein's decision to invade Kuwait and his subsequent refusal to evacuate that country, even as a huge U.S.-orchestrated coalition force massed to evict him, was his conviction that the United States had little stomach for war, that its tolerance for incurring casualties in third world conflicts was low to the point of barring risky military intervention. The chilling effect of the Vietnam War, reinforced by disastrous U.S. military intervention in Lebanon, persuaded Saddam that the United States was not prepared to risk a desert Vietnam.[80]

Osama bin Laden, at least through 9/11, apparently also believed in American cowardice. To the failed U.S. uses of force in Vietnam and Lebanon that Saddam could cite in 1990, bin Laden could add the failed U.S. use of force in Somalia, the Clinton administration's public agonizing over risking loss of American life to stop Serbia's genocidal policies in Bosnia and Kosovo, and the failure of the Clinton and George W. Bush administrations to retaliate for the al Qaeda attack on the USS *Cole* in the Yemeni port of Aden in October 2000. In his 1996 declaration of war against the United States, bin Laden noted the "false courage" of the United States in permitting a single terrorist attack to compel the withdrawal of U.S. forces from Lebanon in 1983–84. He continued,

> But your most disgraceful case was Somalia, where after vigorous propaganda about the power of the USA and its post cold war leadership of the new world order you moved tens of thousands of international forces, including twenty-eight thousand America soldiers into Somalia. However, when tens of your soldiers were killed in minor battles and one American pilot was dragged in the streets of Mogadishu you left the area carrying disappointment, humiliation, defeat and your dead with you.[81]

A month after the 9/11 attacks, Ayman Zawahri, bin Laden's second in command, again referred to American fecklessness. "People of America, your government is leading you into a losing battle," he declared in a statement released by al Jazeera satellite television. "Remember that your government was defeated in Vietnam, fled in panic from Lebanon, rushed out of Somalia and was slapped across the face in Aden."[82]

Thus in the same way that Anglo–French political appeasement encouraged Hitler's aggression, the evident and continuing influence of the "Vietnam syndrome" on U.S. use of force emboldened Osama bin Laden. We do not know what assumptions bin Laden made about how the United States would respond to the al Qaeda attacks on the World Trade Center and the Pentagon, but he had no reason to anticipate a swift U.S. invasion of Afghanistan that would overthrow the Taliban regime and destroy al Qaeda's Afghan training base. After all, bin Laden had played a role in turning Afghanistan into another superpower's Vietnam, and the Taliban had an ally in Pakistan, without whose cooperation the United States could not hope to project its power into Afghanistan. Thus bin Laden may have miscalculated the U.S. response to 9/11, just as Hitler did the Anglo–French reaction to his invasion of Poland. Both bin Laden and Hitler judged their enemies on the basis of past behavior and believed they could count on the same behavior in the future, but their enemies had unwittingly misled bin Laden and Hitler into believing that they were predictable when in fact they were not. This is the stuff of which war by miscalculation is made. Had Britain and France behaved in September 1939 as they had in September 1938 (Munich), March 1938 (Austria's annexation), and March 1936 (the Rhineland's reoccupation), Hitler could have had Poland without general war. And had the United States approached the use of force in September 2001 as it had during the preceding fifteen years (the exception being the Gulf War of 1991), Osama bin Laden might have gotten away with the 9/11 attacks at the cost of a spasm of U.S. air and missile strikes in Afghanistan.

The 9/11 attacks provoked powerful U.S. military responses against Afghanistan and Iraq as well as the formulation of a national security doctrine that emphasized preventive use of force to defeat rising security threats before they fully mature. Osama bin Laden may have terminated the Vietnam syndrome as an inhibiting influence on U.S. use of force. By initiating war directly against the United States and killing three thousand Americans in the process, he enraged and united the country to a degree not witnessed since the Japanese attack on Pearl Harbor. Though that unity eventually dissipated, the Bush administration's robust willingness to use force in Afghanistan and Iraq, supported by a declaratory national security strategy calling for preventive military action against rising security threats, constitutes, for the United States, a reputational role reversal from that of the gun-shy giant of the post-Vietnam decades. Hesitation has given way to intimidation.

Whether this new embrace of force will enhance America's security in the long run remains to be seen. The anticipated swift and politically decisive military win in Iraq did not materialize; instead the United States encountered an unexpected, protracted, and bloody insurgency, prompting critics of the Bush administration to invoke the specter of Vietnam. Osama bin Laden and his allies surely wished to impose another Vietnam on the United States, just as the mujahideen (and their American allies) had imposed upon the Soviet Union a "Vietnam" in Afghanistan. The 9/11 terrorist attacks may have momentarily swept away the constraints of the "Vietnam syndrome" on the use of force, though Secretary of State Colin Powell remained as wary of war with Iraq in 2003 as he was, as chairman of the Joint Chiefs of Staff, in 1991. But a botched occupation and counterinsurgent war in Iraq could establish a new "Iraq syndrome" with just as chilling an effect on American considerations of force as those exerted by the Vietnam War.[83]

At a minimum, the Iraq War exhibits the limits of American military power, with perhaps quite unfortunate consequences. "Consider the prestige that the U.S. military had in the year 2000 and compare it with its standing now," wrote Owen Harries in July 2005.

Then, U.S. military power was universally considered to be awesome in its scope and irresistible in its application. Today, after its deployment in Iraq, the world is much more aware of its limitations and less impressed: aware that while it has enormous capacity to crush and destroy, its ability to control, to impose and maintain order is far less; that while its technology is superb, the human resources at its disposal for protracted occupation or multiple engagements is seriously limited, and the quality of its civilian and military leadership questionable. The U.S.'s military prestige—and therefore its ability to impose its will without recourse to force—has been seriously diminished by Iraq. This will encourage rather than deter its potential enemies.[84]

Concluding Observations
and
Recommendations

WHAT CAN ONE TAKE AWAY from the foregoing assessment of the myths and lessons of appeasing Hitler? I offer the following concluding observations and recommendations:

1. Nazi Germany remains without equal as a state threat.

No post-1945 foreign dictatorship bears genuine comparison to the dictatorship of Adolf Hitler. The scope of Hitler's nihilism, recklessness, and military power and the unlimited scope of his territorial and racial ambitions posed a mortal threat to Western civilization, and there was nothing inevitable about his ultimate defeat. No other authoritarian or totalitarian regime managed to employ such a powerful military instrument in such an aggressive manner to fulfill such a horrendous agenda. Stalin, whose vast crimes were reserved largely for his associates and the peoples of the Soviet Union, had great military power but was cautious and patient; he was a realist and neither lusted for war nor discounted the strength and will of the Soviet Union's enemies. He did not push Moscow's territorial ambitions much beyond the lines gained by Soviet forces at the close of World War II. He was, unlike Hitler, both deterrable and deterred. Mao Zedong, also a domestic political monster, was less cautious but militarily weak. The Korean War taught him the limits of China's power, and he was eventually double contained by the United States and the Soviet Union. Ho Chi Minh and Saddam Hussein were small potatoes compared to Stalin and Mao. Ho's ambitions were limited and his fighting power local, and Saddam was never in a position to overthrow U.S. military domination of the Persian Gulf. And if Ho was undeterrable in his quest for a reunified Vietnam under Communist auspices (a fact that escaped proponents of U.S. military intervention), Saddam proved vulnerable to credible deterrence because he always loved himself more than he hated the United States. Who but Hitler was so powerful and so unappeasable and so undeterrable?

2. American presidents should cease invocation of the Munich analogy to justify threatened or actual uses of force.

Robert Merry properly observes that the word "appeasement" carries "a lot of historical freight, given that for decades it has described the soft and accommodative policies of Britain's Neville Chamberlain toward Adolf Hitler in the 1930s. Thus it suggests that if we don't get tough with any particular regional power, we are going to have another Hitler on our hands." Merry also rightly warns, however, that "not every regional power with national ambitions constitutes a threat to world peace (although it might to American hegemony), and in fact policies based on that assumption are likely to be more destabilizing to peace than such countries themselves."[1] As a strategic threat, Saddam Hussein was hardly Adolf Hitler. Indeed, if anything good can be said about Saddam Hussein, perhaps it is that he did not permit Iraq to degenerate into the world's primary recruiting and training ground for Islamic terrorism.

Invocations of Munich inherently mislead because they ignore the peerlessness of Nazi Germany as a state threat and because they are hardly germane to the emerging strategic environment of proliferating nonstate threats. Though the analogy's power as a tool of opinion mobilization is undeniable, none of America's enemies since 1945 has in fact possessed Nazi Germany's combination military might and willingness—indeed, eagerness—to employ it for unlimited conquest. This does not mean the United States should withhold resort to force against lesser threats. Nor does it mean that Hitlerian threats are a phenomenon of the past. An al Qaeda armed with deliverable nuclear weapons or usable biological weapons would pose a direct and much more lethal threat to the United States than Nazi Germany ever did.

The problem with the Munich analogy is that it reinforces the presidential tendency since 1945 to overstate threats for the purpose of rallying public and congressional opinion, and overstated threats encourage resort to force in circumstances where nonuse of force might better serve long-term U.S. security interests. Threats that are in fact limited tend to be portrayed in Manichaean terms, thus skewing the policy choice toward military action, including preventive military action with all its attendant risks and penalties. If the 1930s reveal the danger of underestimating a security threat, the post–World War II decades contain examples of the danger of overestimating a security threat.

This, to repeat, does not mean that the United States should reserve use of force for only Hitlerian threats. For the United States, limited war has been the rule and total war the exception. As the world's great power, the United States cannot and should not permit limited threats to its own or its allies' security to persist unchallenged even if that means resorting to coercive diplomacy or war. There are of course no guarantees against mistaken war, especially in situations in which both the enemy threat and U.S. interests are limited, the enemy has a significantly greater stake in the outcome of combat than the United States, and sustained public and congressional support for war is questionable. But far worse than the risks of a mistaken decision for war would be to embrace a policy that abjured threatened and actual war as a policy option against all but a direct and overwhelming threat to the United States itself. To do so would be to repeat France's strategic paralysis during the 1930s.

3. Today's strategic environment bears little analogy to that of the 1930s.

The world of the 1930s was a Eurocentric one in which a relatively few powerful and warring states dominated the international system and served as the primary threats to international peace and security. These states waged conventional war against each other on a mass industrial scale and employed their military superiority to rule or coerce Africa and the non-Western regions of the Eurasian land mass. It was a pre-nuclear, unglobalized world of nearly absolute state sovereignty and monopoly of violence, and of no strategically consequential nonstate actors. It was also a world in which the United States was withdrawn from the Eurasian mainland's political and military affairs.

Today's strategic environment could not be more different. Post-1945 imperial disintegration quadrupled the number of states in the international system, and although the state remains the primary actor on the international stage, its sovereignty and power has been weakened by globalization, the rise of influential nonstate actors, and lost monopoly of violence. Weak and failing states have largely displaced powerful ones as the primary source of threats to international peace and security, and irregular warfare within states has largely deposed big conventional wars among states as the primary means of global violence. Europe, once the cockpit of interstate war, has become a zone of seemingly perpetual peace, and the United States, a secondary political and military actor overseas during the 1930s, has achieved an historically unprecedented measure of global power and influence. Perhaps most significant has been the proliferation of nuclear, chemical, and biological weapons to otherwise weak states and the *prospect* of their unprecedented proliferation to undeterrable terrorist organizations. The Bush administration has correctly identified this prospect as the gravest potential threat to U.S. security. Small nonstate organizations in possession of mass destructive capacity heretofore monopolized by states pose a direct threat to the international state system itself; indeed, al Qaeda, which has no analog in the 1930s, seeks to establish a global caliphate, which would entail dissolution of the state system.

That said, it would be erroneous to conclude that the 1930s offer no instruction to early twenty-first-century American policymakers. Principles of statecraft, such as keeping one's objectives within reach of one's means, are enduring, and the fact that the British and French mistakes of the 1930s are now glaringly apparent is no insurance against their being repeated by successor great powers.

4. Osama bin Laden and Adolf Hitler share key traits.

The fundamental disparities between the strategic environments of the 1930s and the first decade of the twenty-first century reduce the usefulness of the Munich analogy, but they do not automatically abort meaningful comparisons of Hitler and bin Laden. On the contrary, though the differences between the German dictator and the Arab terrorist are obvious, the similarities are impressive. Hitler was a secular German state leader obsessed with race, while bin Laden is an Arab nonstate actor obsessed with religion, but both are linked by bloodthirstiness, high intelligence, totalitarian mindset, iron will, fanatical ideological motivation, political charisma, superb tactical skills, and utter ruthlessness and hatefulness. Fortunately for the world, bin Laden does not have at his disposal the state resources that Hitler was able to draw upon or—so far—the destructive power of nuclear weapons (a technological race Hitler lost to the United States).

But the most important trait linking the two men is their *undeterrability*. Like Hitler, bin Laden can be stopped only by assassination or war. Yet it is impossible to envisage Nazi Germany without Hitler—Hitler was the Nazi state. It is, unfortunately, almost certainly the case that al Qaeda and its organizational and inspirational affiliates will survive the death or capture of bin Laden. Hitler presided over a rigidly hierarchical political party and state that were utterly dependent on his leadership; in contrast, Islamic terrorism directed and inspired by al Qaeda is essentially a decentralized transnational insurgency that is more or less immune to catastrophic decapitation. Notwithstanding the loss of its territorial base in Afghanistan and the death or capture of many of its leaders, al Qaeda has demonstrated remarkable powers of regeneration and transmutation—far more so than Nazi Germany was capable of. As such, and because it practices irregular warfare, lacks the exposed assets of a state, and enjoys a measure of regional popularity in the Arab world that was denied to Hitler in Europe, al Qaeda is a much more difficult enemy to destroy than was Nazi Germany, which, unlike al Qaeda, was vulnerable to decisive military defeat.

5. *British and French security choices in the 1930s were neither simple nor obvious.*

The democracies' choices in the 1930s were severely constrained by war weariness, domestic politics, fiscal and economic considerations, perceptions of military inadequacy, and Hitler's effective strategic deception regarding Nazi Germany's intentions and capabilities.

Appeasement of attempted German revision of the Versailles Treaty made both moral and strategic sense because the treaty was unjust, strategically short-sighted, and unenforceable. And it was not politically possible for the democracies to forcibly oppose the reunification of the German nation within a single state. The victors of 1918 had violated Woodrow Wilson's sacred principle of self-determination by prohibiting union of Germany and Austria and by creating the polyglot state of Czechoslovakia with unhappy German majorities in that state's border areas with Germany. Appeasement became untenable the moment Hitler demanded, under the threat of force, the dismemberment of Czechoslovakia—which was not only a democratic state prepared to grant the Sudeten Germans considerable political autonomy but also a significant military counterweight to German territorial ambitions in eastern and southeastern Europe. Yet neither Britain nor France was in a political or military position to defend Czechoslovakia, although Chamberlain's threat of a general war deterred Hitler from seizing all of Czechoslovakia.

Security policy decisions are not made in a political and strategic vacuum; all are contextual and made by fallible human beings who can and do make mistaken judgments based on bad information, poor reasoning, ideological bias, disbelief, fear, overconfidence, stubbornness, and pride. Chamberlain clearly misjudged Hitler, but so did a lot of others, including conservative German nationalists who supported Hitler until his war-ensuring revolutionary intentions became apparent.

6. *Hindsight is not 20/20 vision; it distorts.*

Knowing now what Britain and France (and for that matter the United States) *should* have done in the 1930s—regime change in Berlin via Hitler's assassination or, failing that, an invasion of the Third Reich—is possible only because we know that World War II and the Holocaust were the consequences of appeasement. But these facts were hardly self-evident at the time. Today's retrospective *should* runs afoul of yesterday's actual *could not* and *would not*. British and French statesmen did not know they were on the certain road to general war; on the contrary, they were seeking to avoid war. In any case, neither the assassination of the head of a major European state nor the launching of preventive war against that state fell within the repertory of practical and politically acceptable policy options available to London and Paris. Past events are viewed through the lens of subsequent events. To be sure, Chamberlain profoundly misjudged Hitler and persisted in that misjudgment against accumulating contrary evidence. But had Hitler dropped dead the day after the Munich conference, that conference in all likelihood would be an historical footnote and "appeasement" a nonpejorative term.

As World War II and the Holocaust determined judgment on the wisdom of appeasement, so too will future events in Iraq and the Middle East influence judgment on the wisdom of the Iraq War. As of this writing, a strong case can be made that the Iraq War was a mistake. Discredited "liberation scenario" assumptions, nonexistent Iraqi WMD, no evidence of a collaborative Baathist–al Qaeda relationship, manifest lack of adequate planning for post-Baathist Iraq, botched occupation decisions, continuing Iraqi political turmoil, unexpected and persistent insurgent violence against U.S. forces and Iraqi reconstruction targets, and above all, U.S. casualties surpassing twenty-two hundred dead and sixteen thousand wounded (as of early January 2006) have all combined to erode public support for the war and convince a majority of Americans that the war was a mistake.

Things could look quite different ten or even five years hence, however. The Bush administration believes that Islamic terrorism is rooted in failed governance in the Arab world. Accordingly, it seeks to foster the establishment in Iraq of an economically vibrant democracy, which it believes could serve as a beacon for the political transformation of the rest of the Middle East, which in turn could dry up a major wellspring of Islamic terrorism. This is admittedly a very ambitious strategic bet, premised as it is on American competence in overseas democracy building, an Iraqi national polity of sufficient cultural and political cohesion to embrace and sustain genuine democracy, the regional domino effect of political revolution in Iraq, and Islamic terrorism's incapacity to survive the Arab world's democratization.

But what if the United States wins that strategic bet? What if the decision to invade Iraq in 2003 ends up producing a benign, globalized, democratic Iraq serving as the foundation for profound political and economic change in such autocracies as Egypt, Syria, Saudi Arabia, and Iran? Who then would be prepared to dismiss the Iraq War as a mistake or failure? Who then would care that the decision for war was based on the false assumptions regarding Saddam Hussein's weaponry and relationship to al Qaeda? History will pass judgment on the wisdom of invading Iraq in 2003 just as it passed judgment on the wisdom of appeasement in the 1930s.

7. *The United States is poorly served by reliance on preventive war as a means of dealing with states it fears or simply does not like.*

From the end of World War II until the early 1950s some in the U.S. national security establishment called for war to prevent the Soviet Union from acquiring nuclear weapons. Proponents argued that war with Communist Russia was inevitable and that the United States should attack while it enjoyed a monopoly (or, after 1949, crushing superiority) of nuclear weapons. These calls prompted President Harry Truman to fire the commandant of the U.S. Air War College in Montgomery, Alabama, for publicly urging nuclear attack on the Soviet Union. Truman made a radio address in which he denounced preventive war. "We do not believe in aggression or preventive war," he said. "Such a war is the weapon of dictators, not of free democratic countries like the United States."[2]

Preventive war (as opposed to preemptive military action to defeat an imminent attack) is indistinguishable from aggression, violates the central norm of international politics, alienates real and potential friends and allies, establishes an awful precedent for others to follow, and presumes both war's inevitability with the target state and a level of certain knowledge of target state intentions and capabilities that is rarely obtainable in the real world. The U.S. decision to invade Iraq alienated allies and much of world opinion that had come to appreciate the reassuring restraint with which the United States had used its military power during the cold war and especially its aftermath. The decision was also predicated on false convictions regarding Saddam Hussein's possession of weapons of mass destruction (WMD) and the relationship between Iraq and al Qaeda. (Absent the postulated threats of Iraq's WMD and "alliance" with al Qaeda, the declared aim of Iraq's political transformation was not sufficient to mobilize American public and congressional opinion for war.) Preventive war on behalf of regime change in the third world invites unintended consequences of the kind the United States has encountered in Iraq: complete administrative collapse of the old regime, mounting insurgent resistance to occupation, open-ended war and reconstruction costs, global strategic overstretch, and failed deterrent effect on other rogue-state nuclear weapons aspirations.

True, an emphatic "yes" answers the question of whether the world is better off without Saddam Hussein, but the question itself is hardly relevant. As Richard Haass notes, it "would be akin in a business setting to looking only at revenues and ignoring expenses. What matters in business as well as in foreign policy is the balance or relationship between costs and benefits. It is this assessment that leads to the judgment that the war against Iraq was unwarranted."[3]

The alternative to preventive war as a means of securing the United States from attacks by states armed with WMD is the very policy we successfully pursued against the Soviet

Union during the cold war: nuclear deterrence. To be sure, deterrence has little utility against al Qaeda and other fanatical nonstate actors that present little in the way of vital assets that can be held hostage to the threat of devastating retaliation. For deterrence to work, threatened retaliation must be credible—that is, the deteree must be persuaded that the deterer has the capacity and will to inflict unacceptable retaliatory damage. And because the success of deterrence is measured by events that do not happen (the attack that never materialized), one can never be sure of the cause and effect relationship. That said, there is little reason to believe that rogue states, which like all states have territory, population, military forces, economic assets, and governmental infrastructure that can be held hostage to retaliation, are immune to the logic of nuclear deterrence. Saddam Hussein used WMD only against enemies who were in no position to inflict unacceptable retaliation—Kurdish villagers and Iranian infantry during the 1980s. He refrained from using WMD against enemies who were ready and able to inflict such retaliation—Israel and the United States during the Gulf War. Indeed, no rogue state in possession of WMD has ever employed them against a credible retaliatory state. The one circumstance in which a rogue state would be most likely to do so would be in a regime-change assault that persuaded the leadership that it was doomed to destruction—the Hitler-in-his-bunker scenario—and therefore had nothing to lose by launching its WMD.

The policy choice is between preventive war to thwart rogue state *acquisition* of nuclear weapons versus nuclear deterrence of their *use* once acquired. The admitted challenges of sustaining credible deterrence must be judged against the risks and penalties of preventive war, which have been on painful display ever since the United States convinced itself that no rogue state could have legitimate defensive reasons for acquiring WMD (such as deterring a U.S. attack) and that a horrific Iraqi assault on the United States or U.S. interests overseas was inevitable—and acted accordingly. Strategist Colin Gray argues convincingly that the United States has no practical choice other than to make of deterrence all that it can be, albeit in some seemingly unpromising situations. If this view is rejected, the grim implication is that the United States, as sheriff of the world order, will require heroic performance from those policy instruments charged with cutting edge duties on behalf of preemptive or preventive military operations. Preemption or prevention have their obvious attractions as contrasted with deterrence, at least when they work. But they carry the risk of encouraging a hopeless quest for total security. In order for it to be sensible to regard preemption as an occasional stratagem, rather than as the operational concept of choice, it is essential that the United States wring whatever effectiveness it can out of a strategy of deterrence.[4]

Nuclear proliferation specialist Jeffrey Knopf warns,

Those who seek to write epitaphs for deterrence and containment do so prematurely. Analysis of the relevant logic and available evidence shows that rogue states are not necessarily beyond the reach of deterrence, even in a world where they might be tempted to use terrorist networks to conduct a sneak attack. Those who sweepingly dismiss deterrence and containment as relics of the 20th century thus do a disservice to U.S. national security. They make it less likely that the United States would consider using these tools when they might be effective, even though those tools might help the country avoid some of the costs and risks associated with war. . . . However much the world has changed [since 9/11], the requirements for making sound policy decisions have not. Inferences drawn from a single past event cannot substitute for proper policy analysis—no matter how recent and traumatic the event, and no matter how compelling the lessons of that event feel in its aftermath.[5]

Interestingly, Condoleezza Rice, just a year before she became national security adviser, voiced confidence in nuclear deterrence as the best means of dealing with Saddam Hussein's Iraq and other rogue states. In January 2000 she published an article in *Foreign Affairs* in which she declared "the first line of defense should be a clear and classical statement of deterrence—if they do acquire WMD, their weapons will be unusable because to use them would bring national obliteration." She added that rogue states "were living on borrowed time" and that "there should be no sense of panic about them."[6]

The continuing utility of properly tailored deterrence and containment in dealing with aggressive states does not of course extend to al Qaeda and other terrorist groups with which the United States is already at war. The Bush administration has rightly identified the marriage of terrorism and nuclear and biological weapons as the greatest national security threat facing the United States. War is the only policy choice against undeterrable nonstate enemies seeking mass destructive capacity heretofore available only to states.

8. Political-military coordination is essential to effective statecraft, particularly in overseas state building.

France's failure during the 1930s to harmonize its foreign policy and military capacity contributed significantly to Hitler's prewar diplomatic and territorial triumphs. The French military was neither organizationally nor doctrinally prepared to undertake the kind of operations that would have secured France's security objectives in Europe, especially in central and eastern Europe. Similarly, it is now clear, in the fourth year of America's occupation of Iraq, that there is a serious disconnect between the U.S. objective of securing Iraq's political and economic reconstruction and the U.S. government's lack of preparation to accomplish that objective. To be sure, state building in post-Baathist Iraq would have been a difficult challenge even had the United States been properly prepared for it. But the United States was not prepared for it in large measure because only one federal agency, the Department of Defense, was fully engaged and that agency did not possess the skills to deal with many of the problems that arose with the abrupt and utter political and administrative collapse of the Baathist regime.

The U.S. government did not employ its established interagency process as it approached war with Iraq. The White House, confident in the Department of Defense and seemingly blind to the inherent difficulties of converting military victories into enduring political successes, assigned to the Pentagon virtually the entire responsibility for not only toppling Saddam Hussein but also establishing postwar security and facilitating Iraq's political and economic reconstruction. In turn, the Defense Department, which, like the White House, was convinced that Operation Iraqi Freedom would be a "liberation scenario" entailing a rapid and conclusive termination of hostilities and permitting early establishment of a stable Iraqi political authority and attendant quick drawdown of U.S. forces in Iraq, excluded from the planning process other federal departments, most importantly the State Department and the considerable expertise it had assembled on Iraq. This shutout, which was a function of the bureaucratic and ideological hostility of the DOD's senior civilian leadership to the State Department and the unwillingness or inability of the national security adviser to insist on adherence to the interagency process, might have been less consequential had the liberation scenario materialized instead of the "occupation/insurgency" scenario that did.[7] In fact, the very department of government that had proudly achieved an impressive integration of its once bitterly fractious armed services for the purposes of planning and executing military operations refused to countenance its own integration with the rest of the government for the purpose of political success in Iraq.

Even supporters of the Iraq War have been highly critical on this point. Anthony Cordesman, in the first comprehensive assessment of the Iraq War, concluded that the "National Security Council failed to perform its mission. It acted largely in an advisory role and did not force effective interagency coordination." The exclusion of the State Department, which a year before the launching of Operation Iraqi Freedom had initiated a planning effort to prepare for post-Baathist Iraq—the Future of Iraq Project—was a recipe for a self-inflicted wound because the "Office of the Secretary of Defense staffed its nation-building effort as a largely closed group of members who had strong ideological beliefs but limited practical experience and serious area expertise." The Office of the Secretary of Defense was convinced that "the coalition would have strong popular support from the Iraqis, that other agencies were exaggerating the risks, that the task of nation-building could be quickly transferred to the equivalent of a government in exile, and that the United States and its allies would be able to withdraw quickly."[8] Larry Diamond, who served as senior adviser to the Coalition Provisional Authority in Baghdad, contends that once the decision for war had been made the White House made "two ill-fated decisions" that "squandered victory" in Iraq: (1) it accepted the DOD's plan to go into Iraq "with a relatively light force of about 150,000 Coalition troops, despite the warnings of U.S. Army and outside experts on postconflict reconstruction that—whatever the needs of the war itself—securing the peace would require a force two to three times that size," and (2) it "gave the Pentagon the lead responsibility for the management of postwar Iraq."[9]

One hopes that the American experience in post-Baathist Iraq will serve as a deterrent to future attempted circumventions of the interagency process. Iraq demonstrates the particularly severe penalties of uncoordinated political and military performance with respect to overseas state building. Though the interagency process by no means guarantees successful policy outcomes, it reduces the risk of disastrous policy miscalculation and implementation in very much the same way that jointness within the Department of Defense reduces the risk of military failure. Perhaps the time has come for legislation that would do for the federal government as a whole what the Goldwater-Nichols legislation (the Defense Reorganization Act of 1986) did for the U.S. military.[10]

9. *The prevalence of operations other than warfare (OOTW) over conventional military operations in the post-Soviet world argues strongly for the creation of OOTW-dedicated U.S. military forces.*

America's conventional military primacy has contributed to an evolving strategic environment in which unconventional security threats and tasks have supplanted conventional ones. Yet conventional warfare remains the Defense Department's professional comfort zone; with the exception of the Marine Corps, the armed services, especially the army, have viewed OOTW as unpleasant diversions from the primary and preferred task of preparation for conventional military operations. This outlook is becoming less sustainable with the rise of weak states and nonstate entities as the primary security threats and with each encounter with irregular military enemies. How many more Somalias, Bosnias, Kosovos, 9/11s, Afghanistans, and insurgent Iraqs will it take before the Pentagon begins to transform U.S. military power toward congruency with the deconventionalized strategic environment of the twenty-first century?

This is not a call for converting U.S. land power into the kind of imperial policing force that the British army became during the nineteenth century; that army proved woefully inadequate for the great European conventional war that began in 1914. The United States must retain ground forces capable of prevailing over conventional enemies in kind. But is it not time to consider the establishment of ground forces sized, equipped, organized, and trained specifically for OOTW? The 2005 Rand study cited above calls for improving the counterinsurgency skills of existing U.S. ground forces for possibly creating in the army a dedicated cadre of counterinsurgency specialists and a program to produce such specialists. But is that enough? Do not strategic circumstances argue strongly for the creation of forces dedicated to OOTW and nothing else? To be sure, such forces would not be available for standard conventional military missions. Nor would such forces require the kind of capitalization that has showered so many big-ticket procurement program dollars on congressional districts and the Pentagon, creating powerful vested interests against change. OOTW-dedicated forces would be expensive precisely because they would be manpower- rather than capital-intensive—this raises yet another major question: Should

OOTW-dedicated forces be converted from existing forces or added to them?

There is a limit to how much elasticity can be built into what were once called "general purpose forces"—that is, forces optimized for conventional military operations against a large conventional military foe but sufficiently flexible (or believed to be) to prevail against lesser, irregular enemies. Today the United States faces no conventional military foe but rather an array of actual and potential adversaries dedicated to asymmetrical combat ranging from low-tech insurgency (Iraq) and terrorism (al Qaeda) to high-tech missile and underwater attacks (China) and even nuclear use (North Korea). No single force structure could possibly be optimized to deal with all of these asymmetrical challenges. For example, forces and weapons optimized to deal with China's trans-Taiwan Strait theater ballistic missile and quiet diesel submarine threats would be of little or no use against an Iraq-like insurgency; conversely, infantry maximized for counterinsurgency operations would contribute nothing to Taiwan's defense. Resource constraints exacerbate already difficult force structural choices. "What we need for conventional victory is different from what we need for fighting insurgents, and fighting insurgents has relatively little connection to stopping the spread of nuclear weapons. We can't afford it all," observes defense analyst Loren Thompson.[11]

The issue is hardly simplified by talk of "capabilities-based" force planning as opposed to threat-based force planning. The multiplicity and unpredictability of post–cold war threats to U.S. security and the inherent desirability of certain military capabilities such as strategic mobility and precision strike do not combine to excuse force planning from the necessary effort, however difficult, to identify and prioritize specific threats and build forces to deal with them. There is always the risk of getting it wrong, as did the French in the 1930s, but effective force planning cannot be conducted in a strategic vacuum; it is inescapably informed by a priori judgments of what forces are expected to do. "DOD claims to have moved beyond 'scenario-based planning' to a more enlightened approach called 'capabilities-based planning.' This is said to allow planners to assess alternative

forces without having to be tied to rigidly defined sce-
narios," notes an International Institute for Strategic
Studies assessment. "But it has never been clear how to
gain a sense of what sorts of capabilities are called for
without specifying, at some level, what sorts of operations the forces are prepared to carry out and under what
sorts of conditions."

*10. A significant increase in the size of U.S. ground
forces is in order.*

OOTW are inherently more manpower-intensive than
high-tech conventional warfare, as the U.S. experience in
Iraq has demonstrated. And if OOTW are going to continue
to constitute the primary demand on U.S. ground forces,
then the case for expanded ground forces would seem un-
assailable. Ongoing operations in Iraq and Afghanistan have
depressed ground force recruiting and retention and de-
pleted the land power strategic reserve.

Given the controversy that has arisen over the issue of
ground force size in Iraq and within overall U.S. forces structure, a commission to assess these matters, appointed jointly
by the White House and Congress, should be established.
The commission should also be tasked, should it determine
that significantly expanded land power is required, to assess the best ways of obtaining and sustaining that expansion. A return to conscription seems most unlikely, given
its political unpopularity, and fiscal constraints would seem
to limit severely the option of financing expansion through
increased defense expenditure. The remaining option would
be to move money to the army from the other services—
specifically from air force and navy procurement and re-
search and development programs. Such transfers, however,
would jeopardize realization of transformed conventional
military capabilities (including the army's); this accounts
in large measure for the Pentagon's opposition to expanded
U.S. land power.

But how much conventional military deterrence is
enough—and at what price? During the 1950s the United
States financed a huge investment in air force bomber-based
nuclear deterrence at the expense of conventional force
readiness for nonnuclear threats to U.S. security. Are we

now financing conventional warfare perfection at the expense of forces calibrated for dealing with the unconventional threats that have dominated since the Soviet Union's demise? During the 1950s the air force's bomber-based nuclear deterrent and supporting forces consumed almost half the defense budget; today the army's share of the defense budget is about 24 percent, less than that of either the air force (30 percent) or the navy/Marine Corps (29 percent).[12] If the emerging strategic environment places a premium on ground force–intensive OOTW and if the primary performer of OOTW remains the army, then should not budgetary resources be moved from the airpower and naval power accounts to the land power account, assuming that fiscal constraints preclude any significant increase in defense expenditure?

11. A new and comprehensive assessment of the state of U.S. homeland security is also in order.

We are now five years away from the 9/11 attacks and four years from the creation of the Department of Homeland Security. It is far from self-evident that the giant new bureaucracy combining twenty-two federal agencies and employing 180,000 people has significantly improved homeland security. The absence of additional al Qaeda attacks since 9/11 may reflect a shift in al Qaeda strategy rather than improved security. The security of commercial air travel has unquestionably improved since then, but the jury remains out on such key areas as intelligence and warning, border and surface transportation (especially mass rail) security, critical infrastructure protection, defense against catastrophic threats, and emergency preparedness and response. Against an enemy like al Qaeda and its affiliates, vulnerability invites attack, and it is time to take stock of where we stand on the defensive side of the war on terrorism. Unlike the offensive side of the war, the defensive side involves the coordinated effort of federal, state, and local authorities; it also involves federal funding of state and local agencies performing such key functions as emergency preparedness and response.

The public interest would be well served by a commission on the state of homeland security jointly appointed by the White House and Congress. The commission would examine both the performance of the Department of Homeland Security as well as the status of the key homeland security components cited above.

It is incumbent upon today's U.S. foreign policy decision makers to recognize that the decade of the 1930s offers many important strategic lessons, not just the lesson that aggression unchecked is aggression further encouraged. The British and French mistakes of the 1930s were hardly peculiar to that decade; they can and have been repeated by other great powers. And we should not forget Hitler's mistakes, not the least of which was his failure—indeed, willful refusal—to recognize the limits of German power. Overconfidence is a great power strategic curse that propels into lost wars.

Notes

Chapter 1: Introduction

1. See Jeffrey Record, *Making War, Thinking History: Munich, Vietnam, and Presidential Uses of Force From Korea to Kosovo* (Annapolis, MD: Naval Institute Press, 2002).

2. For an examination of the role the Munich analogy played in the George W. Bush administration's decision to invade Iraq, see Jeffrey Record, "Munich, le Vietnam et l'Irak: Du bon (ou du mauvais) usage de l'histoire," *Politique Etrangere* 70:3 (September 2005): 599–611.

3. Reprinted in "Rhetoric Starts Here," *Washington Post*, November 11, 2002.

4. George W. Bush, "State of the Union Address," January 29, 2002, excerpted in George W. Bush et al., *We Will Prevail: President George W. Bush on War, Terrorism, and Freedom* (New York: Continuum, 2003), 108.

5. For detailed assessments of neoconservative ideology, the rise of neoconservatives to power, and their influence on the foreign policy of the George W. Bush administration, see James Mann, *Rise of the Vulcans: The History of Bush's War Cabinet* (New York: Viking, 2004); Stefan Halper and Jonathan Clarke, *America Alone: The Neo-Conservatives and the Global Order* (New York: Cambridge University Press, 2004); Murray Friedman, *The Neoconservative Revolution: Jewish Intellectuals and the Shaping of Public Policy* (New York: Cambridge University Press, 2005); and Gary Dorrien, *Imperial Designs: Neoconservatism and the New Pax Americana* (New York: Routledge, 2005).

6. Andrew J. Bacevich, *The New American Militarism: How Americans Are Seduced by War* (New York: Oxford University Press, 2005), 73.

7. Bush, *We Will Prevail*, 6.

8. Harry S. Truman, *Memoirs*, Vol. 2, *Years of Trial and Hope, 1946–1952* (Garden City, NY: Doubleday, 1955–56), 335.

9. Dwight Eisenhower, letter to Winston Churchill, 1954, excerpted in Robert J. MacMahon, ed., *Major Problems in the History of the Vietnam War*, 2nd ed. (Lexington, MA: D. C. Heath, 1995), 373.

10. Quoted in Theodore C. Sorenson, *Kennedy* (New York: Harper and Row, 1965), 703.

11. Doris Kearns, *Lyndon Johnson and the American Dream* (New York: Harper and Row, 1976), 252.

12. Richard Nixon, *The Memoirs of Richard Nixon* (New York: Grosset and Dunlap, 1978), 269–270.

13. Ronald Reagan, "Radio Address to the Nation on Defense Spending," February 19, 1983, in *Public Papers of the Presidents of the United States: Ronald Reagan, 1983* (Washington, DC: U.S. Government Printing Office, 1984), 1:258.

14. George H. W. Bush, "Address to the Nation Announcing the Deployment of United States Armed Forces to Saudi Arabia," August 8, 1990, in *Public Papers of the Presidents of the United States: George Bush, 1990* (Washington, DC: U.S. Government Printing Office, 1991) 2:108.

15. Quoted in "Lessons From the War in Kosovo," *Heritage Foundation Backgrounder*, no. 1311, 5, n.d.

16. George W. Bush, "President Says Saddam Hussein Must Leave Iraq Within 48 Hours," March 17, 2003, http://www.whitehouse.gov/news/releases/2003/03/20030317-7.html.

17. See Record, *Making War, Thinking History*.

18. Stephen R. Rock, *Appeasement in International Politics* (Lexington: University Press of Kentucky, 2000), 5.

19. Robert Jervis, *Perception and Misperception in International Politics* (Princeton: Princeton University Press, 1976), 90.

20. Jean-Baptiste Duroselle, *France and the Nazi Threat: The Collapse of French Diplomacy, 1932–1939* (New York: Enigma Books, 2004), 155–156.

21. Frank McDonough, *The Origins of the First and Second World Wars* (New York: Cambridge University Press, 1997), 96.

22. Harry Hearder, "Editor's Forward," in P. M. H. Bell, *The Origins of the Second World War in Europe*, 2nd ed. (London: Longman Group, 1997), viii.

23. David M. Potter, *The Impending Crisis 1848–1861* (New York: Harper and Row, 1976), 145.

24. Robert J. Young, *France and the Origins of the Second World War* (New York: St. Martin's Press, 1996), 108.

25. *Webster's New World Dictionary and Thesaurus*, 2nd ed. (New York: Hungry Minds, 2002.), 27–28.

26. Rock, *Appeasement in International Politics*, 12.

27. Gordon A. Craig and Alexander L. George, *Force and Statecraft: Diplomatic Problems of Our Time*, 2nd ed. (New York: Oxford University Press, 1990), 250.

28. Paul Kennedy, *The Rise and Fall of the Great Powers: Economic Change and Military Conflict From 1500 to 2000* (New York: Random House, 1987), 16, 39.

29. See Rock, *Appeasement in International Politics*, 25–47.

Chapter 2: Why Britain and France Appeased Hitler

1. Edmund Stillman and William Pfaff, *The Politics of Hysteria: The Sources of Twentieth-Century Conflict* (New York: Harper and Row, 1964), 115–121.

2. McDonough, *Origins of the First and Second World Wars*, 43.

3. Bell, *Origins of the Second World War*, 11.

4. Williamson Murray, "Appeasement and Intelligence," *Intelligence and National Security* 2:4 (October 1987): 48–49.

5. Benjamin F. Martin, *France in 1938* (Baton Rouge: Louisiana State University Press, 2005), 17.

6. A. J. P. Taylor, *The Origins of the Second World War* (London: Hamish Hamilton, 1961), 68–72. Also see pp. 105–109.

7. See Gordon Martel, ed., *The Origins of the Second World War Reconsidered: A. J. P. Taylor and the Historians*, 2nd ed. (London: Routledge, 1999).

8. See McDonough, *Origins of the First and Second World Wars*, 92–93; and Bell, *Origins of the Second World War*, 50–52.

9. Joachim Fest, *Inside Hitler's Bunker: The Last Days of the Third Reich* (New York: Farrar, Straus and Giroux, 2004), 41.

10. Both the 1941 and 1945 statements quoted in ibid., 130.

11. Norman Rich, *Hitler's War Aims: Ideology, the Nazi State, and the Course of Expansion* (New York: W. W. Norton, 1973), 4.

12. Margaret MacMillan, *Paris 1919: Six Months That Changed the World* (New York: Random House, 2001), 493.

13. Gerhard L. Weinberg, *Germany, Hitler, and World War II: Essays in Modern German and World History* (New York: Cambridge University Press, 1995), 30.

14. For a concise discussion of how Hitler saw the world, see ibid., 30–53.

15. Bell, *Origins of the Second World War*, 94.

16. Leon Goldensohn, *The Nuremberg Interviews: An American Psychiatrist's Conversations With Defendants and Witnesses*, ed. Robert Gellately (New York: Alfred A. Knopf, 2004), 223–224.

17. Richard Overy, "Misjudging Hitler: A. J. P. Taylor and the Third Reich," in Martel, *Origins of the Second World War Reconsidered*.

18. Fest, *Inside Hitler's Bunker*, 40.

19. Ronald M. Smelser, "Nazi Dynamics, German Foreign Policy and Appeasement," in *The Fascist Challenge and the Policy of Appeasement*, eds. Wolfgang J. Mommsen and Lothar Kettenecker (London: George Allen and Unwin, 1983), 42.

20. Bell, *Origins of the Second World War*, 28–29; *The Oxford Companion to World War II* (New York: Oxford University Press, 1995),

279; and William L. Shirer, *The Rise and Fall of the Third Reich: A History of Nazi Germany* (New York: Simon & Schuster, 1960), 358.

21. Kennedy, *Rise and Fall of the Great Powers*, 338.

22. On October 3, 1938, Winston Churchill condemned the Munich agreement before the House of Commons. He said that Nazi Germany "cannot ever be the trusted friend of British democracy" because the Nazi regime was one "which spurns Christian ethics, which cheers its onward course by a barbarous paganism, which vaunts the spirit of aggression and conquest, which derives strength and perverted pleasure from persecution, and uses, as we have seen, with pitiless brutality the threat of murderous force." Quoted in Graham Stewart, *Burying Caesar: The Churchill–Chamberlain Rivalry* (New York: Overlook Press, 1999), 346.

23. Donald Cameron Watt, "British Intelligence and the Coming of the Second World War in Europe," in *Knowing One's Enemies: Intelligence Assessment Before the Two World Wars*, ed. Ernest R. May (Princeton: Princeton University Press, 1984), 247.

24. Quoted in Robert Allan Doughty, *The Seeds of Disaster: The Development of French Army Doctrine 1919–1939* (Hamden, CT: Archon Books, 1984), 36, 38.

25. Richard Overy, *The Road to War*, rev. ed., with Andrew Wheatcroft (London: Penguin Books, 1999), 71.

26. Rock, *Appeasement in International Politics*, 174.

27. Andrew J. Crozier, *The Causes of the Second World War* (Malden, MA: Blackwell Publishers, 1997), 12.

28. William R. Rock, "British Appeasement (1930s): A Need for Revision?" *South Atlantic Quarterly* 78:3 (Summer 1979): 294.

29. See Robert J. Young, "French Military Intelligence and Nazi Germany, 1938–1939," in *Knowing One's Enemies*, 271–309.

30. Robert J. Young, *In Command of France: French Foreign Policy and Military Planning, 1933–1940* (Cambridge: Harvard University Press, 1978), 13.

31. See Doughty, *Seeds of Disaster*, 1–40.

32. Eliot A. Cohen and John Gooch, *Military Misfortunes: The Anatomy of Failure in War* (New York: Random House, 1990), 214.

33. For the best assessment of the influence of domestic political and military organizational cultures on France's military posture in the 1930s, see Elizabeth Kier, *Imagining War: French and British Military Doctrine Between the Wars* (Princeton: Princeton University Press, 1997).

34. Ibid., 65.

35. For an examination of the reserve system as a source of French military doctrine and France's defeat in 1940, see Eugenia C. Kiesling, *Arming Against Hitler: France and the Limits of Military Planning* (Lawrence: University Press of Kansas, 1996), 85–135.

36. See Jean Lacouture, *De Gaulle*, vol. 1, *The Rebel 1890–1944*, trans. Patrick O'Brien (New York: W. W. Norton, 1990), 129–148; and Brian Crozier, *De Gaulle* (New York: Charles Scribner's Sons, 1973),

62–69. De Gaulle published his ideas in a small 1934 book, *Toward the Professional Army*, which sold only about 750 copies in France but reportedly more in Germany and the Soviet Union.

37. Kiesling, *Arming Against Hitler*, 117–118, 172.

38. Henry Kissinger, *Diplomacy* (New York: Simon & Schuster, 1994), 303.

39. Quoted in Doughty, *Seeds of Disaster*, 36, 37.

40. Young, *In Command of France*, 58–59.

41. Duroselle, *France and the Nazi Threat*, 189, 190.

42. See Telford Taylor, *Munich: The Price of Peace* (Garden City, NY: Doubleday, 1979), 472–476.

43. See Richard Lamb, *Mussolini as Diplomat: Il Duce's Italy on the World Stage* (New York: Fromm International, 1999), 100–107. Though British diplomacy in the mid-1930s seemingly went out of its way to alienate Mussolini as a strategic partner against Hitler, an alliance between Rome and Berlin was probably inevitable, given the ideological affinities between Nazism and Italian Fascism, especially their shared contempt for bourgeois democracy and Italian imperial ambitions in the Mediterranean and Africa, which could be realized only at the expense of British and French interests.

44. Quoted in Duroselle, *France and the Nazi Threat*, 136.

45. Quoted in Shirer, *Rise and Fall of the Third Reich*, 293.

46. Ibid., 294–295.

47. See Kiesling, *Arming Against Hitler*, 183–187.

48. Quoted in ibid., 186.

49. See discussion in Crozier, *Causes of the Second World War*, 233–245.

50. For an examination of the financial limits and Treasury influence on British rearmament during 1937–39, see N. H. Gibbs, *Grand Strategy*, vol. 1, *Rearmament Policy*, in *History of the Second World War, United Kingdom Military Series*, ed. J. R. M. Butler (London: Her Majesty's Stationery Office, 1976), 279–300.

51. Kennedy, *Rise and Fall of the Great Powers*, 320

52. For an official strategic history of the ten-year rule and its termination, see Gibbs, *Rearmament Policy*, 35–87.

53. Committee of Imperial Defense, "Annual Review by the Chiefs of Staff Sub-Committee," quoted in John Dunabin, "The British Military Establishment and the Policy of Appeasement," in *Fascist Challenge*, 176.

54. Gibbs, *Rearmament Policy*, 94.

55. Quoted in ibid, 259.

56. Quoted in Taylor, *Munich*, 631.

57. Overy, *Road to War*, 104

58. Gibbs, *Rearmament Policy*, 450.

59. For an extensive discussion of the concept of limited liability as formulated by Liddell Hart and the relationship of that concept to Britain's strategic situation in the 1930s, see Azar Gat, *A History of Military Thought: From the Enlightenment to the Cold War* (New York: Oxford University Press, 2001), 696–783.

60. The Franco–Soviet pact of mutual assistance, directed against Germany, was a militarily toothless political alliance because the French refused to hold the military staff talks with their Soviet counterparts necessary to coordinate war plans and because the Soviet Union did not share a border with Germany or enjoy the right of military passage with eastern European states that European states did. Kissinger, *Diplomacy*, 296–297.

61. See Williamson Murray, *The Change in the European Balance of Power, 1938–1939: The Path to Ruin* (Princeton: Princeton University Press, 1984), 84–92.

62. Quoted in Keith Feiling, *The Life of Neville Chamberlain* (London: Macmillan, 1946), 314.

63. Quoted in Gibbs, *Rearmament Policy*, 447.

64. Feiling, *Life of Neville Chamberlain*, 276–278.

65. Bell, *Origins of the Second World War*, 194.

66. See Martin Gilbert and Richard Gott, *The Appeasers* (London: Phoenix Press, 1963), 115; and Richard Meyers, "British Imperial Interests and the Policy of Appeasement," in *Fascist Challenge*, 339.

67. Michael Graham Fry, "Agents and Structures: The Dominions and the Czechoslovak Crisis, September 1938," *Diplomacy and Statecraft* 10:2–3 (July/November 1999): 295.

68. Quoted in Daryl G. Press, "The Credibility of Power: Assessing Threats During the 'Appeasement' Crises of the 1930s," *International Security* 29:3 (Winter 2004–5): 164.

69. Quoted in MacMillan, *Paris 1919*, 32.

70. See Robert Frankenstein, "The Decline of France and the Policy of Appeasement," in *Fascist Challenge*, 236–245.

71. Arthur H. Furnia, *The Diplomacy of Appeasement: Anglo–French Relations and the Prelude to World War II, 1931–1938* (Washington, DC: University Press of Washington, DC, 1960), 388.

72. Young, *France and the Origins of the Second World War*, 247.

73. Martin Thomas, "France and the Czechoslovak Crisis," *Diplomacy and Statecraft* 10:2–3 (July/November 1999): 149.

74. Winston Churchill, *The Gathering Storm* (Boston: Houghton-Mifflin, 1938), 302.

75. Quoted in Duroselle, *France and the Nazi Threat*, 300.

76. Quoted in Martin, *France in 1938*, 158–159.

77. Gerald Guenwook Lee, "'I See Dead People': Air-Raid Phobia and Britain's Behavior in the Munich Crisis," *Security Studies* 13:2 (Winter 2003–4): 266.

78. Murray, "Appeasement and Intelligence," 231; and David Vital, "Czechoslovakia and the Powers: September 1938," *Journal of Contemporary History* 1:4 (October 1966): 44–45.

79. Donald Cameron Watt, *How War Came: The Immediate Origins of the Second World War, 1938–1939* (New York: Pantheon Books, 1989), 195.

80. Murray, "Appeasement and Intelligence," 261. Also see Taylor, *Munich*, 819.

81. Vital, "Czechoslovakia and the Powers," 7. Also see Walter Gorlitz,

ed., *The Memoirs of Field Marshal Wilhelm Keitel*, trans. David Irving (New York: Cooper Square Press, 2000), 62–73.

82. See Klaus-Jurgen Muller, "The German Military Opposition Before the Second World War," in *Fascist Challenge*, 67–70; and Shirer, *Rise and Fall of the Third Reich*, 366–384, and 404–414.

83. See Muller, "German Military Opposition," 67–68; Stewart, *Burying Caesar*, 297; and R. A. C. Parker, *Chamberlain and Appeasement: British Policy and the Coming of the Second World War* (New York: St. Martin's Press, 1993), 153–154.

84. Muller, "German Military Opposition," 70.

85. Ewald von Kleist-Schmenzin, quoted in Taylor, *Munich*, 663.

86. Quoted in Ian Kershaw, *Hitler, 1936–1945: Nemesis* (New York: W. W. Norton, 2000), 88.

87. Taylor, *Munich*, 390–395.

88. Richard Overy, "Germany and the Munich Crisis: A Mutilated Victory?" *Diplomacy and Statecraft* 10:2–3 (July/November 1999): 203.

89. Kershaw, *Hitler*, 122.

90. Ibid., 122; and Overy, "Germany and the Munich Crisis," 209.

91. In June Hitler had told Field Marshal Keitel that he would attack Czechoslovakia "only if I am firmly convinced, as in the case of the demilitarized zone and the entry into Austria, that France will not march, and that therefore Britain will not intervene." Quoted in Churchill, *Gathering Storm*, 290.

92. See Taylor, *Munich*, 878–884; and Parker, *Chamberlain and Appeasement*, 173–176.

93. Parker, *Chamberlain and Appeasement*, 175.

94. Quoted in Taylor, *Munich*, 874.

95. Ibid., 878.

96. Richard Overy, *Interrogations: The Nazi Elite in Allied Hands, 1945* (New York: Penguin, 2001), 316.

97. Overy, *Road to War*, 103.

98. J. W. Wheeler-Bennett, *Munich: Prologue to Tragedy* (New York: Duell, Sloan and Pearce, 1948), 331.

99. Quoted in ibid.

100. Watt, "British Intelligence," 30; Kershaw, *Hitler*, 163–164.

101. Kershaw, *Hitler*, 230.

102. Quoted in Overy, *Road to War*, 57–58.

103. Goldensohn, *Nuremberg Interviews*, 443.

104. Excerpted in Shirer, *Rise and Fall of the Third Reich*, 399.

105. Gerhard L. Weinberg, "Reflections on Munich After 60 Years," *Diplomacy and Statecraft* 10:2–3 (July/November 1999): 8.

106. "I have always believed that Benes was wrong to yield. He should have defended his fortress line. Once the fighting had begun, in my opinion at the time, France would have moved to his aid in a surge of national passion, and Britain would have rallied to France almost immediately." Churchill, *Gathering Storm*, 302.

107. For an account of the decision, see Vital, "Czechoslovakia and the Powers," 60–65.

108. Katriel Ben-Arie, "Czechoslovakia at the Time of 'Munich': The Military Situation," *Journal of Contemporary History* 25 (1990): 444.

109. Kissinger, *Diplomacy*, 242.

110. Parker, *Chamberlain and Appeasement*, 11.

111. Taylor, *Munich*, 76.

112. Kissinger, *Diplomacy*, 242–243.

113. See Gibbs, *Rearmament Policy*, 155–170.

114. Lamb, *Mussolini as Diplomat*, 114.

115. Piers Brendon, *The Dark Valley: A Panorama of the 1930s* (New York: Random House, 2000), 305.

116. Quoted in ibid., 20.

117. See Lee, "Air-Raid Phobia"; and Uri Bialer, *The Shadow of the Bomber: The Fear of Air Attack and British Politics 1932–1939* (London: Royal Historical Society, 1980).

118. Quoted in Gibbs, *Rearmament Policy*, 10.

119. Richard Overy, "Air Power and the Origins of Deterrence Theory Before 1939," *Journal of Strategic Studies* 15:1 (1992): 78–79.

120. Quoted in Wesley K. Wark, *The Ultimate Enemy: British Intelligence and Nazi Germany, 1933–1939* (Ithaca, NY: Cornell University Press, 1985), 28.

121. Tami Davis Biddle, *Rhetoric and Reality in Air Warfare: The Evolution of British and American Ideas About Strategic Bombing, 1914–1945* (Princeton: Princeton University Press, 2002), 112.

122. Ibid., 121; and Taylor, *Munich*, 648.

123. Biddle, *Rhetoric and Reality in Air Warfare*, 111.

124. Taylor, *Munich*, 218.

125. Ibid., 112. In fact, when war broke out in September 1939, Germany's strength in frontline aircraft was 3,609, compared to Britain's 1,911 and France's 1,792. German and British aircraft annual production rates were, however, approaching parity at 8,000. *Oxford Companion to World War II*, 14.

126. Quoted in Taylor, *Munich*, 849.

127. Bell, *Origins of the Second World War*, 202.

128. Ibid., 216.

129. Williamson Murray, "Strategic Bombing: The British, American, and German Experiences," in Williamson Murray and Allan R. Millett, *Military Innovation in the Interwar Period* (New York: Cambridge University Press, 1996), 131.

130. Murray, *Change in the European Balance*, 51.

131. See Robert J. Young, "The Use and Abuse of Fear: France and the Air Menace in the 1930s," *Intelligence and National Security* 2:4 (October 1987): 88–109.

132. Young, *In Command of France*, 288–289.

133. Thomas, "France and the Czechoslovak Crisis," 140–143.

134. See Anthony Christopher Cain, *The Forgotten Air Force: French Doctrine in the 1930s* (Washington, DC: Smithsonian Institution Press, 2002).

135. Taylor, *Munich*, 719.

136. Duroselle, *France and the Nazi Threat*, 278–279.

137. Robert Jervis, "Deterrence and Perception," *International Security* 7:3 (Winter 1982–83): 14, 15.

138. Dominic D. P. Johnson, *Overconfidence and War: The Havoc and Glory of Positive Illusions* (Cambridge: Harvard University Press, 2004), 92.

139. Gibbs, *Rearmament Policy*, 597–600.

140. Ibid., 99.

141. Taylor, *Munich*, 197, 198.

142. Quoted in ibid., 200.

143. Young, *France and the Origins of the Second World War*, 117.

144. See Donald N. Lammers, *Explaining Munich: The Search for Motive in British Policy* (Stanford, CA: Hoover Institution, 1966), 12–15; and A. L. Rowse, *Appeasement: A Study in Political Decline 1933–1939* (New York: W. W. Norton, 1961), 63, 116–118.

145. Quoted in Rowse, *Appeasement*, 82.

146. Ibid., 18.

147. Rich, *Hitler's War Aims*, 238.

148. Before and during the war, Hitler spoke admiringly of America's continental unity (a model for Europe under German control) and machine-based society. See Gerhard L. Weinberg, ed., *Hitler's Second Book: The Unpublished Sequel to* Mein Kampf, trans. Krista Smith (New York: Enigma Books, 2003), 107–110 and 117–118; and *Hitler's Secret Conversations* (New York: Farrar, Straus and Young, 1953), 228, 337.

149. C. A. MacDonald, *The United States, Britain and Appeasement, 1936–1939* (New York: St. Martin's Press, 1981), 50–51, 73, 82–83, 105, 179.

150. In January 1938 the House of Representatives almost passed the Ludlow Amendment, which would have required a national plebiscite to authorize a declaration of war.

151. MacDonald, *United States, Britain and Appeasement*, 182.

152. See Barbara Rearden Franham, *Roosevelt and the Munich Crisis: A Study of Political Decision-Making* (Princeton: Princeton University Press, 1997), 137–172.

153. See David Reynolds, *From Munich to Pearl Harbor: Roosevelt's America and the Origins of the Second World War* (Chicago: Ivan R. Dee, 2001).

154. Bell, *Origins of the Second World War*, 131.

155. Crozier, *Causes of the Second World War*, 155.

156. Young, *France and the Origins of the Second World War*, 94.

157. Lammers, *Explaining Munich*, especially pp. 49–51.

158. Robert J. Beck, "Munich's Lessons Reconsidered," *International Security* 14:2 (Fall 1989): 187.

Chapter 3: Why Appeasement Failed

1. J. L. Richardson, "New Perspectives on Appeasement: Some Implications for International Relations," *World Politics* 40:3 (April 1988): 306.

2. Rich, *Hitler's War Aims*, xlii

3. See "The Hossbach Memorandum: A Strategy Conference?" in *World War II: Roots and Causes*, ed. Keith Eubank (Lexington, MA: D. C. Heath, 1975), 95–106; and E. M. Robertson, *Hitler's Pre-War Policy and Military Plans* (London: Longman's Green, 1963), 106–107.

4. See Robertson, *Hitler's Pre-War Policy*, 181–191.

5. Richardson, "New Perspectives on Appeasement," 67–68.

6. May, *Knowing One's Enemies*, 520.

Chapter 4: Appeasement's Lessons for the United States Today

1. Quoted in Johnson, *Overconfidence and War*, 92.

2. Two detailed studies conclude that Bush administration decision makers did in fact portray various Iraqi WMD threats well beyond the supporting evidence. See Joseph Cirincione, Jessica T. Mathews, George Perkovich, *WMD in Iraq: Evidence and Implications*, with Alexis Norton (Washington, DC: Carnegie Endowment for International Peace, 2004); and John Prados, *Hoodwinked: The Documents That Reveal How Bush Sold Us the War* (New York: New Press, 2004).

3. Letter of transmittal to the president accompanying *Report of the Commission on the Intelligence Capabilities of the United States Regarding Weapons of Mass Destruction* (Washington, DC: March 31, 2005).

4. *Report of the Commission*, 3.

5. Ibid., 4.

6. See the *Final Report of the National Commission on Terrorist Attacks Upon the United States* (New York: W. W. Norton, 2004).

7. See Gil Merom, *How Democracies Lose Small Wars: State, Society, and the Failures of France in Algeria, Israel in Lebanon, and the United States in Vietnam* (New York: Cambridge University Press, 2003); Andrew Mack, "Why Big Nations Lose Small Wars: The Politics of Asymmetric Conflict," *World Politics* 27 (1975): 175–200; and Ivan Arreguin-Toft, *How the Weak Win Wars: A Theory of Asymmetric Conflict* (New York: Cambridge University Press, 2005).

8. See John Mueller, *War, Presidents, and Public Opinion* (New York: John Wiley and Sons, 1973); Eric V. Larsen, *Casualties and Consensus: The Historical Role of Casualties in Domestic Support for U.S. Military Operations* (Santa Monica, CA: Rand Corporation, 1996); and Benjamin C. Schwarz, *Casualties, Public Opinion, and U.S. Military Intervention: Implications for U.S. Regional Deterrence Strategies* (Santa Monica, CA: Rand Corporation, 1994). For assessments of public support for post–Vietnam War U.S. uses of force and the relationship of that support to casualties, see Mark J. Conversino, "Sawdust Superpower: Perceptions of U.S. Casualty Tolerance in the Post–Gulf War Era," *Strategic Review* 14:1 (Winter 1986):15–23; Karl W. Eikenberry, "Take No Casualties,"

Parameters 26:2 (Summer 1996):109–118; Jeffrey Record, *Failed States and Casualty Phobia: Implications for Force Structure and Policy Choices*, Occasional Paper No. 18 (Maxwell Air Force Base, AL: Center for Strategy and Technology, Air University, October 2000); and Robert Sobel, *The Impact of Public Opinion on Foreign Policy Since Vietnam: Constraining the Colossus* (Oxford: Oxford University Press, 1990). For a landmark assessment of American casualty sensitivity and its determinants, see Peter D. Feaver and Christopher Gelpi, *Choosing Your Battles: American Civil-Military Relations and the Use of Force* (Princeton: Princeton University Press, 2004), esp. 95–183.

9. Jeffrey Record and W. Andrew Terrill, *Iraq and Vietnam: Differences, Similarities, and Insights* (Carlisle, PA: Institute for Strategic Studies, U.S. Army War College, May 2004).

10. Joseph Carroll, "The Iraq–Vietnam Comparison," Gallup Poll Tuesday briefing, June 15, 2002, http://poll.gallup.com/content/default.aspx?CI=11998.

11. Larsen, *Casualties and Consensus*, 227–229.

12. Casualty figures for Vietnam based on calculations appearing in Record and Terrill, *Iraq and Vietnam*, 11–12. Casualty figures for Iraq drawn from data appearing in the website *Iraq Coalition Casualty Count* (http://icasualties.org/oif).

13. All polling data taken from *The Gallup Brain: Iraq*, http://institution.gallup.com/com/content/?ci=1633 Last accessed January 4, 2006.

14. Feaver and Gelpi, *Choosing Your Battles*, 149.

15. Though this term is no longer in official usage, I use it here because it accurately separates those lesser tasks the U.S. military has been called upon to perform and the major conventional military operations against like adversaries for which it organizes, equips, and trains to fight.

16. Anthony H. Cordesman, *Iraq and Conflict Termination: The Road to Guerrilla War?* (Washington, DC: Center for Strategic and International Studies, July 23, 2003), 23.

17. Antulio J. Echevarria II, *Toward an American Way of War* (Carlisle, PA: Strategic Studies Institute, U.S. Army War College, March 2004), 10, 16.

18. David J. Lonsdale, *The Nature of War in the Information Age* (New York: Frank Cass, 2004), 9, 211.

19. Frederick W. Kagan, "War and Aftermath," *Policy Review* 120 (August–September 2003): 27.

20. Ibid., 44–45.

21. David C. Hendrickson and Robert W. Tucker, "Revisions in Need of Revising: What Went Wrong in the Iraq War," *Survival* 47:2 (Summer 2005): 27. Also see Eliot A. Cohen, "A Time for Humility," *Wall Street Journal*, January 31, 2005.

22. Colin S. Gray, "How Has War Changed Since the End of the Cold War?" *Parameters* 35:1 (Spring 2005): 21.

23. Max Boot, "The Struggle to Transform the Military," *Foreign Affairs* 84:2 (March–April 2005): 118.

24. See Jeffrey Record, "The Limits and Temptations of America's Conventional Military Primacy," *Survival* 47:1 (Spring 2005): 33–50.

25. Robert D. Kaplan, "How We Would Fight China," *Atlantic Monthly* 295:5 (June 2005): 55.

26. See Jeffrey Record, *The Creeping Irrelevance of U.S. Force Planning* (Carlisle, PA: Strategic Studies Institute, U.S. Army War College, May 1998).

27. Thomas X. Hammes, *The Sling and the Stone: On War in the 21st Century* (St. Paul, MN: Zenith Press, 2004), 3, 5.

28. Stephen Metz and Raymond Millen, *Insurgency and Counterinsurgency in the 21st Century: Reconceptualizing Threat and Response* (Carlisle, PA: Strategic Studies Institute, U.S. Army War College, November 2004), vi.

29. See Robert R. Tomes, "Relearning Counterinsurgency Warfare," *Parameters* 34:1 (Spring 2004): 16–28.

30. See Bruce Hoffman, *Insurgency and Counterinsurgency in Iraq* (Santa Monica, CA: Rand Corporation, June 2004).

31. *Iraq: Translating Lessons Into Future DoD Policies* (Santa Monica, CA: Rand Corporation, February 2005), 7.

32. See Gopal Ratnam, "With QDR, Pentagon Takes Lead in U.S. Strategy," *Defense News*, January 31, 2005, 1; Jason Sherman, "Rumsfeld Shifts QDR's Direction, Broadens Focus on Terrorism, WMD," *Inside the Pentagon*, February 10, 2005, 1; and Greg Jaffe, "Rumsfeld Details Big Military Shift in New Document," *Wall Street Journal*, March 11, 2005.

33. See Lawrence J. Korb, "All-Volunteer Army Shows Signs of Wear," *Atlanta Journal-Constitution*, February 27, 2005; Dave Moniz, "Army Misses Recruiting Goal," *USA Today*, March 3, 2005; Tom Bowman, "Army Worries About Quality," *Baltimore Sun*, March 7, 2005; Dave Moniz, "For Guard Recruiters, A Tough Sell," *USA Today*, March 8, 2005; Mark Mazzetti, "Recruiting Goals Are in Harm's Way," *Los Angeles Times*, March 17, 2005; Morton M. Kondracke, "Army, Marines Need Priority in Rumsfeld's New Defense Review," *Roll Call*, March 17, 2005; and Robert Burns, "Study: Army Stretched to Breaking Point," *Washington Post*, January 24, 2006.

34. Tom Squitieri, "General Says New War Could Strain Military," *USA Today*, February 17, 2005.

35. Richard N. Haass, *The Opportunity: America's Moment to Alter History* (New York: Public Affairs, 2005), 10.

36. *The Military Balance 2004–2005* (London: International Institute for Strategic Studies, 2004), 24, 27; and Boot, "The Struggle to Transform the Military," 107.

37. Boot, "The Struggle to Transform the Military," 108.

38. Korb, "All-Volunteer Force Shows Signs of Wear."

39. Barry R. McCaffrey, "Failure Isn't an Option," *Wall Street Journal*, June 27, 2005.

40. Jonathan Weisman and Renae Merle, "Pentagon Scales Back Arms Plan," *Washington Post*, January 5, 2005.

41. Eric Schmitt and Thom Shanker, "Rumsfeld and Army Want to Delay Decision on Larger Force," *New York Times*, February 9, 2005.

42. See Frederick W. Kagan, "What Rumsfeld's Defenders Don't Want to Admit," *Weekly Standard* 10:17 (January 17, 2005): 19–21.

43. McCaffrey, "Failure Isn't an Option"; Tom Squitieri, "Reserve, Guard Raise Recruiting Age," *USA Today*, March 22, 2005; Dave Moniz, "Army Offers 1&1/4 Year Hitch," *USA Today*, May 13, 2005; and Michelle Cottle, "Draft Pick," *New Republic Online*, June 17, 2005, http://www.tnr.com/doc.mhtml?I=w050613&s=cottle061705.

44. Charles Moskos, "Feel That Draft?" *Chicago Tribune*, June 8, 2005.

45. Quoted in Robert D. Novak, "Iraq and the Recruitment Crisis," *Washington Post*, May 26, 2005.

46. Jeffrey Record, *Bounding the Global War on Terrorism* (Carlisle, PA: Strategic Studies Institute, U.S. Army War College, December 2003).

47. For an extended discussion of this issue, see Jeffrey Record, "Threat Confusion and Its Penalties," *Survival* 46:2 (Summer 2004): 51–72.

48. Robert A. Pape, *Dying to Win: The Strategic Logic of Suicide Terrorism* (New York: Random House, 2005), 6, 246.

49. Douglas Jehl, "Iraq May Be Prime Place for Training of Militants, C.I.A. Report Concludes," *New York Times*, June 22, 2005.

50. Daniel Benjamin and Steven Simon, *The Next Attack: The Failure of the War on Terrorism and a Strategy for Getting It Right* (New York: Henry Holt, 2005), xiv.

51. For critical assessments of U.S. mistakes in Iraq, see David L. Phillips, *Losing Iraq: Inside the Postwar Reconstruction Fiasco* (New York: Westview Press, 2005); Larry Diamond, *Squandered Victory: The American Occupation and the Bungled Effort to Bring Democracy to Iraq* (New York: Henry Holt, 2005); and George Packer, *The Assassin's Gate: America in Iraq* (New York: Farrar, Straus and Giroux, 2005).

52. Stephen D. Biddle, *American Grand Strategy After 9/11: An Assessment* (Carlisle, PA: Strategic Studies Institute, U.S. Army War College, April 2005), 23.

53. Ibid., 9.

54. Zbigniew Brzezinski, *The Choice: Global Domination or Global Leadership* (New York: Basic Books, 2004), 27–28.

55. Eric Schmitt and Thom Shanker, "U.S. Officials Retool Slogan for Terror War," *New York Times*, July 26, 2005; and Sidney Blumenthal, "Selling the War," www.salon.com, July 28, 2005.

56. *Report of the Defense Science Board Task Force on Strategic Communication* (Washington, DC: Department of Defense, September 2004), 40, http://www.acq.osd.mil/dsb/reports/2004-09-Strategic_Communication.pdf.

57. *Strategic Survey 2004/5: An Evaluation and Forecast of World Affairs* (London: International Institute for Strategic Studies, 2005), 8.

58. Fawaz A. Gerges, *The Far Enemy: Why the Jihad Went Global* (New York: Cambridge University Press, 2005), 258.

59. Brzezinski, *Choice*, 31.
60. Record, *Bounding the Global War on Terrorism*, 41.
61. *National Security Strategy*, 28.
62. See Kaplan, "How We Would Fight China"; and Jeffrey Record, "Thinking About War and China," *Aerospace Power Journal* 15:4 (Winter 2001): 69–80.
63. Robert W. Merry, *Sands of Empire: Missionary Zeal, American Foreign Policy, and the Hazards of Global Ambition* (New York: Simon & Schuster, 2005), 242–243.
64. See Kershaw, *Hitler*, 290–291; Ernest R. May, *Strange Victory: Hitler's Conquest of France* (New York: Hill and Wang, 2000), 230–239; and Julian Jackson, *The Fall of France: The Nazi Invasion of 1940* (New York: Oxford University Press, 2003), 330–332.
65. To be sure, during the cold war Soviet strategic nuclear forces directly threatened U.S. territory, but their use was deterred by the threat of overwhelming American retaliation in kind.
66. See Mia Bloom, "Grim Saudi Export—Suicide Bombers," *Los Angeles Times*, July 17, 2005; and Bryan Bender, "Study Cites Seeds of Terror in Iraq," *Boston Globe*, July 17, 2005.
67. Quoted in Bender, "Study Cites Seeds of Terror."
68. Stephen E. Flynn, "The Neglected Home Front," *Foreign Affairs* 83:5 (September–October 2004): 23. Also see Flynn's *America the Vulnerable: How Our Government Is Failing to Protect Us* (New York: HarperCollins, 2004).
69. *Emergency Responders: Drastically Underfunded, Dangerously Unprepared*, Report of an Independent Task Force Sponsored by the Council on Foreign Relations (New York: Council on Foreign Relations, 2003), 1.
70. Eric Lichtblau, "Government Report on U.S. Aviation Warns of Security Holes," *New York Times*, March 14, 2005.
71. "Our Unnecessary Insecurity," *New York Times*, February 20, 2005.
72. Flynn, *America the Vulnerable*, 118–119.
73. See Mimi Hall, "Chemical Plants: Vulnerability at Issue," *USA Today*, April 26, 2005.
74. *Final Report on the 9/11 Commission Recommendations*, December 5, 2005, www.9/11pdp.org, 1, 2.
75. Graham Allison, *Nuclear Terrorism: The Ultimate Preventable Catastrophe* (New York: Henry Holt, 2004), 124, 133.
76. Ibid., 55.
77. Benjamin and Simon, *Next Attack*, 231.
78. The literature on North Korean and Soviet calculations behind the decision to invade South Korea and on the Truman administration's decision to fight is voluminous. See Richard C. Thornton, *Odd Man Out: Truman, Mao, and the Origins of the Korean War* (Washington, DC: Brassey's, Inc., 2000); Sergei N. Goncharov, John W. Lewis, and Xue Litai, *Uncertain Partners: Stalin, Mao, and the Korean War* (Stanford, CA: Stanford University Press, 1993); William Stueck, *Rethinking the Korean War: A New Diplomatic and Strategic History* (Princeton: Princeton University Press, 2002),

1–83; Alexander L. George and Richard Smoke, *Deterrence in American Foreign Policy: Theory and Practice* (New York: Columbia University Press, 1974), 140–234; John Lewis Gaddis, "Korea in American Politics, Strategy, and Diplomacy, 1945–50," in *The Origins of the Cold War in Asia*, eds. Yonosuke Nagai and Akira Iriye (New York: Columbia University Press, 1977), 277–298; James I. Matray, "Korea: Test Case of Containment in Asia," in *Child of Conflict: The Korean American Relationship, 1943–1953*, ed. Bruce Cumings (Seattle: University of Washington Press, 1983), 169–193; H. A. DeWeerd, "Strategic Surprise in the Korean War," *Orbis* 6:3 (Fall 1962): 435–452; Stephen Pelz, "U.S. Decisions on Korean Policy, 1943–1950: Some Hypotheses," in Cumings, *Child of Conflict*, 93–132; Barton J. Bernstein, "The Week We Went to War: American Intervention in the Korean Civil War," *Foreign Service Journal* 54:1 (January 1977): 6–34; and Dean Acheson, "Relations of the Peoples of the United States and the Peoples of Asia," *Vital Speeches of the Day* 16:8 (February 1, 1950): 238–244.

79. See Janice Gross Stein, "Deterrence and Compellance in the Gulf, 1990–91," *International Security* 17:2 (Fall 1992): 147–179; and "Iraqi Transcript of the Hussein-Glaspie Meeting" (July 25, 1990), in *The Middle East*, 7th ed. (Washington, DC: Congressional Quarterly, 1991), 360–381.

80. See Norman Cigar, "Iraq's Strategic Mindset and the Gulf War: Blueprint for Defeat," *Journal of Strategic Studies* 15:1 (March 1992): 2–14; and Jeffrey Record, "Defeating Desert Storm (and Why Saddam Didn't)," *Comparative Strategy*, April–June 1993, 125–140.

81. "Declaration of War Against the Americans Occupying the Land of the Two Holy Places," *Al Quds Al Arabi*, August 1996. Reprinted in *Online News Hour With Jim Lehrer*, http://www.pbs.org/newshour/terrorism/international/fatwa_1996.html.

82. Statements by Osama bin Laden and his lieutenants released by al Jazeera satellite TV, October 10, 2001, http://www.ict.org.il/spotlight/det.cfm?id=688.

83. See John Mueller, "The Iraq Syndrome," *Foreign Affairs* 84:6 (November–December 2005): 44–54.

84. Owen Harries, "Costs of a Needless War," *The Australian*, July 18, 2005.

Chapter 5: Concluding Observations and Recommendations

1. Merry, *Sands of Empire*, 170.

2. Excerpted from "Text of Truman's 'Report to the Nation' on the Korean War," *New York Times*, September 2, 1950.

3. Haass, *Opportunity*, 189.

4. Colin S. Gray, *Maintaining Effective Deterrence* (Carlisle, PA: Strategic Studies Institute, U.S. Army War College, August 2003), 10.

5. Jeffrey W. Knopf, "Misapplied Lessons? 9/11 and the Iraq Debate," *Non-Proliferation Review* 9:2 (Fall–Winter 2002): 65.

6. Condoleezza Rice, "Promoting the National Interest," *Foreign Affairs* 79:1 (January–February 2000): 61.

7. Phillips, *Losing Iraq*, 55–65.

8. Anthony H. Cordesman, *The Iraq War: Strategy, Tactics, and Military Lessons* (Washington, DC: Center for Strategic and International Studies, 2003), 498. Also see David Rothkopf, *Running the World: The Inside Story of the National Security Council and the Architects of American Power* (New York: Basic Books, 2005), 389–441.

9. Diamond, *Squandered Victory*, 280.

10. See Martin J. Gorman and Alexander Krongrad, "A Goldwater-Nichols Act for the U.S. Government: Institutionalizing the Interagency Process," *Joint Forces Quarterly* 39 (2005): 51–58; and Donald R. Drechsler, "Reconstructing the Interagency Process After Iraq," *Journal of Strategic Studies*, February 2005, 3–30.

11. Quoted in Thom Shanker and Eric Schmitt, "Pentagon Weighs Strategy Change to Deter Terror," *New York Times*, July 5, 2005.

12. For analysis of U.S. defense spending trends during the 1950s see Jeffrey Record, *Revising U.S. Military Strategy: Tailoring Means to Ends* (Washington, DC: Pergamon-Brassey's, 1984), 13–2. Data on today's spending by service appears in *Military Balance 2004–2005*, 261–265.

Bibliography

Acheson, Dean. "Relations of the Peoples of the United States and the Peoples of Asia." *Vital Speeches of the Day* 16:8 (February 1, 1950): 238–244.

Allison, Graham. *Nuclear Terrorism: The Ultimate Preventable Catastrophe*. New York: Henry Holt, 2004.

Arreguin-Toft. "How the Weak Win Wars." *International Security* 26:1 (Summer 2001): 93–128.

———. *How the Weak Win Wars: A Theory of Asymmetric Conflict*. New York: Cambridge University Press, 2005.

Bacevich, Andrew. *The New American Militarism: How Americans Are Seduced by War*. New York: Oxford University Press, 2005.

Beck, Robert J. "Munich's Lessons Reconsidered." *International Security* 14:2 (Fall 1989): 161–191.

Bell, P. M. H. *The Origins of the Second World War in Europe*. 2nd ed. London: Longman Group, 1997.

Ben-Arie, Katriel. "Czechoslovakia at the Time of 'Munich': The Military Situation." *Journal of Contemporary History* 25 (1990): 430–446.

Bender, Bryan. "Study Cites Seeds of Terror in Iraq." *Boston Globe*, July 17, 2005.

Benjamin, Daniel, and Steven Simon. *The Next Attack: The Failure of the War on Terrorism and a Strategy for Getting It Right*. New York: Henry Holt, 2005.

Bernstein, Barton J. "The Week We Went to War: American Intervention in the Korean Civil War." *Foreign Service Journal* 54:1 (January 1977): 6–34.

Beschloss, Michael, ed. *Taking Charge: The Johnson White House Tapes, 1963–1964*. New York: Simon & Schuster, 1997.

Bialer, Uri. *The Shadow of the Bomber: The Fear of Air Attack and British Politics 1932–1939*. London: Royal Historical Society, 1980.

Biddle, Stephen D. *American Grand Strategy After 9/11: An Assessment*.

Carlisle, PA: Strategic Studies Institute, U.S. Army War College, April 2005.

Biddle, Tami Davis. *Rhetoric and Reality in Air Warfare: The Evolution of British and American Ideas About Strategic Bombing, 1914–1945*. Princeton: Princeton University Press, 2002.

Bloom, Mia. "Grim Saudi Export—Suicide Bombers." *Los Angeles Times*, July 17, 2005.

Blumenthal, Sidney. "Selling the War." www.salon.com, July 28, 2005.

Boot, Max. "The Struggle to Transform the Military." *Foreign Affairs* 84:2 (March–April 2005): 103–118

Bowman, Tom. "Army Worries About Quality." *Baltimore Sun*, March 7, 2005.

Brendon, Piers. *The Dark Valley: A Panorama of the 1930s*. New York: Random House, 2000.

Brzezinski, Zbigniew. *The Choice: Global Domination or Global Leadership*. New York: Basic Books, 2004.

Burns, Robert. "Study: Army Stretched to Breaking Point." *Washington Post*, January 24, 2006.

Bush, George H. W. *Public Papers of the Presidents of the United States: George Bush, 1990*. Vol. 2. Washington, DC: U.S. Government Printing Office, 1991.

Bush, George W., et al. *We Will Prevail: President George W. Bush on War, Terrorism, and Freedom*. New York: Continuum, 2003.

Cain, Anthony Christopher. *The Forgotten Air Force: French Doctrine in the 1930s*. Washington, DC: Smithsonian Institution Press, 2002.

Churchill, Winston. *The Gathering Storm*. Boston: Houghton-Mifflin, 1948.

Cigar, Norman. "Iraq's Strategic Mindset and the Gulf War: Blueprint for Defeat." *Journal of Strategic Studies* 15:1 (March 1992): 2–14.

Cirincione, Joseph, Jessica T. Matthews, and George Perkovich. *WMD in Iraq: Evidence and Implications*. With Alexis Norton. Washington, DC: Carnegie Endowment for International Peace, 2004.

Cohen, Eliot A. "A Time for Humility." *Wall Street Journal*, January 31, 2005.

Cohen, Eliot A., and John Gooch. *Military Misfortunes: The Anatomy of Failure in War*. New York: Random House, 1990.

Conversino, Mark J. "Sawdust Superpower: Perceptions of U.S. Casualty Tolerance in the Post–Gulf War Era." *Strategic Review* 14:1 (Winter 1986): 15–23.

Cordesman, Anthony H. *Iraq and Conflict Termination: The Road to Guerrilla War?* Washington, DC: Center for Strategic and International Studies, July 23, 2003.

Cottle, Michelle. "Draft Pick." *New Republic Online*, June 17, 2005. http://www.tnr.com/doc.mhtm?I=w050613&s=cottle061705.

Craig, Gordon A., and Alexander L. George. *Force and Statecraft: Diplomatic Problems of Our Time*. 2nd ed. New York: Oxford University Press, 1990.

Crozier, Andrew J. *The Causes of the Second World War*. Malden, MA: Blackwell Publishers, 1997.

Crozier, Brian. *De Gaulle*. New York: Charles Scribner's Sons, 1973.

Cumings, Bruce, ed. *Child of Conflict: The Korean American Relationship, 1943–1953.* Seattle: University of Washington Press, 1983. "Declaration of War Against the Americans Occupying the Land of the Two Holy Places." *Al Quds Al Arabi*, August 1996. Reprinted in *Online News Hour With Jim Lehrer.* http://www.pbs.org/newshour/terrorism/international/fatwa_1996.html.

DeWeerd, H. A. "Strategic Surprise in the Korean War." *Orbis* 6:3 (Fall 1962): 435–452.

Diamond, Larry. *Squandered Victory: The American Occupation and the Bungled Effort to Bring Democracy to Iraq.* New York: Henry Holt, 2005.

Dorrien, Gary. *Imperial Designs: Neoconservatism and the New Pax Americana.* New York: Routledge, 2005.

Doughty, Robert Allan. *The Seeds of Disaster: The Development of French Army Doctrine 1919–1939.* Hamden, CT: Archon Books, 1984.

Duroselle, Jean-Baptiste. *France and the Nazi Threat: The Collapse of French Diplomacy, 1932–1939.* New York: Enigma Books, 2004.

Echevarria, Antulio J., II. *Toward an American Way of War.* Carlisle, PA: Strategic Studies Institute, U.S. Army War College, March 2004.

Eikenberry, Karl W. "Take No Casualties." *Parameters* 26:2 (Summer 1996): 109–118.

Emergency Responders: Drastically Underfunded, Dangerously Unprepared. Report of an Independent Task Force Sponsored by the Council on Foreign Relations. New York: Council on Foreign Relations, 2003.

Feaver, Peter D., and Christopher Gelpi. *Choosing Your Battles: American Civil-Military Relations and the Use of Force.* Princeton: Princeton University Press, 2004.

Feiling, Keith. *The Life of Neville Chamberlain.* London: Macmillan, 1946.

Fest, Joachim. *Inside Hitler's Bunker: The Last Days of the Third Reich.* New York: Farrar, Straus and Giroux, 2004.

Final Report of the National Commission on Terrorist Attacks Upon the United States. New York: W. W. Norton, 2004.

Final Report on the 9/11 Commission Recommendations, December 5, 2005. www.9/11pdp.org.

Flynn, Stephen E. *America the Vulnerable: How Our Government Is Failing to Protect Us.* New York: HarperCollins, 2004.

———. "The Neglected Home Front." *Foreign Affairs* 83:5 (September–October 2004): 20–33.

Franham, Barbara Reardon. *Roosevelt and the Munich Crisis: A Study of Political Decision-Making.* Princeton: Princeton University Press, 1997.

Frankenstein, Robert. "The Decline of France and the Policy of Appeasement." In Mommsen and Kettenecker, *Fascist Challenge.*

Friedman, Murray. *The Neoconservative Revolution: Jewish Intellectuals and the Shaping of Public Policy.* New York: Cambridge University Press, 2005.

Fry, Michael Graham. "Agents and Structures: The Dominions and the Czechoslovak Crisis, September 1938." *Diplomacy and Statecraft* 10:2–3 (July/November 1999): 293–341.

Furnia, Arthur H. *The Diplomacy of Appeasement: Anglo–French Relations and the Prelude to World War II, 1931–1938*. Washington, DC: University Press of Washington, DC, 1960.

Gaddis, John Lewis. "Korea in American Politics, Strategy, and Diplomacy, 1945–50." In *The Origins of the Cold War in Asia*. Edited by Yonosuke Nagai and Akira Iriye. New York: Columbia University Press, 1977.

Gat, Azar. *A History of Military Thought: From the Enlightenment to the Cold War*. New York: Oxford University Press, 2001.

George, Alexander L., and Richard Smoke. *Deterrence in American Foreign Policy: Theory and Practice*. New York: Columbia University Press, 1974.

Gerges, Fawaz A. *The Far Enemy: Why the Jihad Went Global*. New York: Cambridge University Press, 2005.

Gibbs, N. H. *Grand Strategy*. Vol. 1, *Rearmament Policy*. In *History of the Second World War, United Kingdom Military Series*. Edited by J. R. M. Butler. London: Her Majesty's Stationery Office, 1976.

Gilbert, Martin, and Richard Gott. *The Appeasers*. London: Phoenix Press, 1963.

Goldensohn, Leon. *The Nuremberg Interviews: An American Psychiatrist's Conversations With Defendants and Witnesses*. Edited and introduced by Robert Gellately. New York: Alfred A. Knopf, 2004.

Goncharov, Sergei N., John W. Lewis, and Xue Litai. *Uncertain Partners: Stalin, Mao, and the Korean War*. Stanford, CA: Stanford University Press, 1993.

Gorlitz, Walter, ed. *The Memoirs of Field Marshal Wilhelm Keitel*. Translated by David Irving. New York: Cooper Square Press, 2000.

Gray, Colin S. "How Has War Changed Since the End of the Cold War?" *Parameters* 35:1 (Spring 2005): 14–26.

———. *Maintaining Effective Deterrence*. Carlisle, PA: Strategic Studies Institute, U.S. Army War College, August 2003.

Haass, Richard N. *The Opportunity: America's Moment to Alter History*. New York: Public Affairs, 2005.

Hall, Mimi. "Chemical Plants: Vulnerability at Issue." *USA Today*, April 26, 2005.

Halper, Stefan, and Jonathan Clarke. *America Alone: The Neo-Conservatives and the Global Order*. New York: Cambridge University Press, 2004.

Hammes, Thomas X. *The Sling and the Stone: On War in the 21st Century*. St. Paul, MN: Zenith Press, 2004.

Harries, Owen. "Costs of a Needless War." *The Australian*, July 18, 2005.

Hendrickson, David C., and Robert W. Tucker. "Revisions in Need of Revising: What Went Wrong in the Iraq War." *Survival* 47:2 (Summer 2005): 7–32.

Hitler's Secret Conversations. New York: Farrar, Straus and Young, 1953.

Hoffman, Bruce. *Insurgency and Counterinsurgency in Iraq*. Santa Monica, CA: Rand Corporation, June 2004.

"The Hossbach Memorandum: A Strategy Conference?" In *World War II:*

Roots and Causes. Edited by Keith Eubank. Lexington, MA: D. C. Heath, 1975.

Iraq: Translating Lessons Into Future DoD Policies. Santa Monica, CA: Rand Corporation, February 2005.

"Iraqi Transcript of the Hussein-Glaspie Meeting." *The Middle East*. 7th ed. Washington, DC: Congressional Quarterly, 1991.

Jackson, Julian. *The Fall of France: The Nazi Invasion of 1940*. New York: Oxford University Press, 2003.

Jaffe, Greg. "Rumsfeld Details Big Military Shift in New Document." *Wall Street Journal*, March 11, 2005.

Jehl, Douglas. "Iraq May Be Prime Place for Training of Militants, C.I.A. Report Concludes." *New York Times*, June 22, 2005.

Jervis, Robert. "Deterrence and Perception." *International Security* 7:3 (Winter 1982–83): 3–30.

———. *Perception and Misperception in International Politics*. Princeton: Princeton University Press, 1976.

Johnson, Dominic D. P. *Overconfidence and War: The Havoc and Glory of Positive Illusions*. Cambridge: Harvard University Press, 2004.

Kagan, Donald. *On the Origins of War and the Preservation of Peace*. New York: Anchor Books, 1995.

Kagan, Frederick W. "War and Aftermath." *Policy Review* 120 (August–September 2003): 3–27.

———. "What Rumsfeld's Defenders Don't Want to Admit." *Weekly Standard* 10:17 (January 17, 2005): 19–21.

Kaplan, Robert D. "How We Would Fight China." *Atlantic Monthly* 295:5 (June 2005): 49–64.

Kearns, Doris. *Lyndon Johnson and the American Dream*. New York: Harper and Row, 1976.

Kennedy, Paul. *The Rise and Fall of the Great Powers: Economic Change and Military Conflict From 1500 to 2000*. New York: Random House, 1987.

Kershaw, Ian. *Hitler, 1936–1945: Nemesis*. New York: W. W. Norton, 2000.

Kier, Elizabeth. *Imagining War: French and British Military Doctrine Between the Wars*. Princeton: Princeton University Press, 1997.

Kiesling, Eugenia C. *Arming Against Hitler: France and the Limits of Military Planning*. Lawrence: University Press of Kansas, 1996.

Kissinger, Henry. *Diplomacy*. New York: Simon & Schuster, 1994.

Knopf, Jeffrey W. "Misapplied Lessons? 9/11 and the Iraq Debate." *Non-Proliferation Review* 9:2 (Fall–Winter 2002): 47–66.

Kondracke, Morton M. "Army, Marines Need Priority in Rumsfeld's New Defense Review." *Roll Call*, March 17, 2005.

Korb, Lawrence J. "All-Volunteer Force Shows Signs of Wear." *Atlanta Journal-Constitution*, February 27, 2005.

Lacouture, Jean. *De Gaulle*. Vol. 1, *The Rebel 1890–1944*. Translated by Patrick O'Brien. New York: W. W. Norton, 1990.

Lamb, Richard. *Mussolini as Diplomat: Il Duce's Italy on the World Stage*. New York: Fromm International, 1999.

Lammers, Donald N. *Explaining Munich: The Search for Motive in British Policy*. Stanford, CA: Hoover Institution, 1966.

Larsen, Eric. *Casualties and Consensus: The Historical Role of Casualties in Domestic Support for U.S. Military Operations*. Santa Monica, CA: Rand Corporation, 1996.

Lee, Gerald Guenwook. "'I See Dead People': Air-Raid Phobia and Britain's Behavior in the Munich Crisis." *Security Studies* 13:2 (Winter 2003–4): 230–272.

"Lessons From the War in Kosovo." *Heritage Foundation Backgrounder* No. 1311, n.d.

Lichtblau, Eric. "Government Report of U.S. Aviation Warns of Security Holes." *New York Times*, March 14, 2005.

Lonsdale, David J. *The Nature of War in the Information Age*. New York: Frank Cass, 2004.

MacDonald, C. A. *The United States, Britain and Appeasement, 1936–1939*. New York: St. Martin's Press, 1981.

Mack, Andrew. "Why Big Nations Lose Small Wars: The Politics of Asymmetric Conflict." *World Politics* 27 (1975): 175–200.

MacMahon, Robert J., ed. *Major Problems in the History of the Vietnam War*. 2nd ed. Lexington, MA: D. C. Heath, 1995.

MacMillan, Margaret. *Paris 1919: Six Months That Changed the World*. New York: Random House, 2001.

Mann, James. *Rise of the Vulcans: The History of Bush's War Cabinet*. New York: Viking, 2004.

Martel, Gordon, ed. *The Origins of the Second World War Reconsidered: A. J. P. Taylor and the Historians*. 2nd ed. London: Routledge, 1999.

Martin, Benjamin F. *France in 1938*. Baton Rouge: Louisiana State University Press, 2005.

Matray, James I. "Korea: Test Case of Containment in Asia." In Cumings, *Child of Conflict*.

May, Ernest R. *Knowing One's Enemies: Intelligence Assessment Before the Two World Wars*. Princeton: Princeton University Press, 1984.

———. *Strange Victory: Hitler's Conquest of France*. New York: Hill and Wang, 2000.

Mazzetti, Mark. "Recruiting Goals Are in Harm's Way." *Los Angeles Times*, March 17, 2005.

McCaffrey, Barry R. "Failure Isn't an Option." *Wall Street Journal*, June 27, 2005.

McDonough, Frank. *The Origins of the First and Second World Wars*. New York: Cambridge University Press, 1997.

Merom, Gil. *How Democracies Lose Small Wars: State, Society, and the Failures of France in Algeria, Israel in Lebanon, and the United States in Vietnam*. New York: Cambridge University Press, 2003.

Merry, Robert W. *Sands of Empire: Missionary Zeal, American Foreign Policy, and the Hazards of Global Ambition*. New York: Simon & Schuster, 2005.

Metz, Stephen, and Raymond Millen. *Insurgency and Counterinsurgency in the 21st Century: Reconceptualizing Threat and Response*. Carlisle, PA: Strategic Studies Institute, U.S. Army War College, November 2004.

Meyers, Richard. "British Imperial Interests and the Policy of Appeasement." In Mommsen and Kettenecker, *Fascist Challenge*.

The Military Balance 2004–2005. London: International Institute for Strategic Studies, 2004.

Mommsen, Wolfgang J., and Lothar Kettenecker, eds. *The Fascist Challenge and the Policy of Appeasement*. London: George Allen and Unwin, 1983.

Moniz, Dave. "Army Misses Recruiting Goal." *USA Today*, March 3, 2005.

———. "Army Offers 1&1/4 Year Hitch." *USA Today*, May 13, 2005.

———. "For Guard Recruiters, A Tough Sell." *USA Today*, March 8, 2005.

Moskos, Charles. "Feel That Draft?" *Chicago Tribune*, June 8, 2005.

Mueller, John. "The Iraq Syndrome." *Foreign Affairs* 84:6 (November–December 2005): 44–54.

———. *War, Presidents, and Public Opinion*. New York: John Wiley and Sons, 1973.

Muller, Klaus-Jurgen. "The German Military Opposition Before the Second World War." In Mommsen and Kettenecker, *Fascist Challenge*.

Murray, Williamson. "Appeasement and Intelligence." *Intelligence and National Security* 2:4 (October 1987): 47–66.

———. *The Change in the European Balance of Power, 1938–1939: The Path to Ruin*. Princeton: Princeton University Press, 1984.

———. "Strategic Bombing: The British, American, and German Experiences." In Williamson Murray and Allan R. Millett, *Military Innovation in the Interwar Period*. New York: Cambridge University Press, 1996.

Nixon, Richard. *The Memoirs of Richard Nixon*. New York: Grosset and Dunlap, 1978.

Novak, Robert D. "Iraq and the Recruitment Crisis." *Washington Post*, May 26, 2005.

"Our Unnecessary Insecurity." *New York Times*, February 20, 2005.

Overy, Richard. "Air Power and the Origins of Deterrence Theory Before 1939." *Journal of Strategic Studies* 15:1 (1992): 73–101.

———. "Germany and the Munich Crisis: A Mutilated Victory?" *Diplomacy and Statecraft* 10: 2–3 (July–November 1999): 191–215.

———. *Interrogations: The Nazi Elite in Allied Hands, 1945*. New York: Penguin, 2001.

———. "Misjudging Hitler: A. J. P. Taylor and the Third Reich." In Martel, *Origins of the Second World War Reconsidered*.

———. *The Road to War*. Revised ed. With Andrew Wheatcroft. London: Penguin Books, 1999.

The Oxford Companion to World War II. New York: Oxford University Press, 1995.

Packer, George. *The Assassin's Gate: America in Iraq*. New York: Farrar, Straus and Giroux, 2005.

Pape, Robert A. *Dying to Win: The Strategic Logic of Suicide Terrorism*. New York: Random House, 2005.

Parker, R. A. C. *Chamberlain and Appeasement: British Policy and the Coming of the Second World War*. New York: St. Martin's Press, 1993.

Pelz, Stephen. "U.S. Decisions on Korean Policy, 1943–1950: Some Hypotheses." In Cumings, *Child of Conflict*.

Phillips, David L. *Losing Iraq: Inside the Postwar Reconstruction Fiasco*. New York: Westview Press, 2005.

Prados, John. *Hoodwinked: The Documents That Reveal How Bush Sold Us the War*. New York: New Press, 2004.

Potter, David M. *The Impending Crisis 1848–1861*. New York: Harper and Row, 1976.

"President Says Saddam Hussein Must Leave Iraq Within 28 Hours." http://www.whitehouse.gov/news/releases/2003/03/20020317-7.html.

Press, Daryl G. "The Credibility of Power: Assessing Threats During the 'Appeasement' Crises of the 1930s." *International Security* 29:3 (Winter 2004–5): 136–169.

Ratnam, Gopal. "With QDR, Pentagon Takes Lead in U.S. Strategy." *Defense News*, January 31, 2005.

Reagan, Ronald. *Public Papers of the Presidents of the United States: Ronald Reagan, 1983*. Vol. 1. Washington, DC: U.S. Government Printing Office, 1984.

Record, Jeffrey. *Bounding the Global War on Terrorism*. Carlisle, PA: Strategic Studies Institute, U.S. Army War College, December 2003.

———. *The Creeping Irrelevance of U.S. Force Planning*. Carlisle, PA: Strategic Studies Institute, U.S. Army War College, May 1998.

———. "Defeating Desert Storm (and Why Saddam Didn't)." *Comparative Strategy*, April–June 1993, 125–140.

———. *Failed States and Casualty Phobia: Implications for Force Structure and Policy Choices*. Occasional Paper No. 18. Maxwell Air Force Base, AL: Center for Strategy and Technology, Air University, October 2000.

———. "The Limits and Temptations of America's Conventional Military Primacy." *Survival* 47:1 (Spring 2005): 33–50.

———. *Making War, Thinking History: Munich, Vietnam, and Presidential Uses of Force From Korea to Kosovo*. Annapolis, MD: Naval Institute Press, 2002.

———. "Munich, le Vietnam et l'Irak: Du bon (ou du mauvais) usage de l'histoire." *Politique Etrangere* 70:3 (September 2005): 599–611.

———. "Thinking About War and China." *Aerospace Power Journal* 15:4 (Winter 2001): 69–80.

———. "Threat Confusion and Its Penalties." *Survival* 46:2 (Summer 2004): 51–72.

Record, Jeffrey, and W. Andrew Terrill. *Iraq and Vietnam: Differences, Similarities, and Insights*. Carlisle, PA: Institute for Strategic Studies, U.S. Army War College, May 2004.

Report of the Commission on the Intelligence Capabilities of the United States Regarding Weapons of Mass Destruction. Washington, DC, March 31, 2005.

Report of the Defense Science Board Task Force on Strategic Communication, Washington, DC: Department of Defense, September 2004. http://www.acq.osd.mil/dsb/reports/2004-09-StrategicCommunication.pdf .

Reynolds, David. *From Munich to Pearl Harbor: Roosevelt's America and the Origins of the Second World War.* Chicago: Ivan R. Dee, 2001.

"Rhetoric Starts Here." *Washington Post,* November 11, 2002.

Rice, Condoleezza. "Promoting the National Interest." *Foreign Affairs* 79:1 (January–February 2000): 45–62.

Rich, Norman. *Hitler's War Aims: Ideology, the Nazi State, and the Course of Expansion.* New York: W. W. Norton, 1973.

Richardson, J. L. "New Perspectives on Appeasement: Some Implications for International Relations." *World Politics* 40:3 (April 1988): 289–316.

Robertson, E. M. *Hitler's Pre-War Policy and Military Plans.* London: Longman's Green, 1963.

Rock, Stephen R. *Appeasement in International Politics.* Lexington: University Press of Kentucky, 2000.

Rock, William R. "British Appeasement (1930s): A Need for Revision?" *South Atlantic Quarterly* 78:3 (Summer 1979): 290–301.

Rowse, A. L. *Appeasement: A Study in Political Decline 1933–1939.* New York: W. W. Norton, 1961.

Schmitt, Eric, and Thom Shanker. "Rumsfeld and Army Want to Delay Decision on Larger Force." *New York Times,* February 9, 2005.

———. "U.S. Officials Retool Slogan for Terror War." *New York Times,* July 26, 2005.

Schwarz, Benjamin C. *Casualties, Public Opinion, and U.S. Military Intervention: Implications for U.S. Regional Deterrence Strategies.* Santa Monica, CA: Rand Corporation, 1994.

Sherman, Jason. "Rumsfeld Shifts QDR's Direction, Broadens Focus on Terrorism, WMD." *Inside the Pentagon,* February 10, 2005.

Shirer, William L. *The Rise and Fall of the Third Reich: A History of Nazi Germany.* New York: Simon & Schuster, 1960.

Smelser, Ronald M. "Nazi Dynamics, German Foreign Policy and Appeasement." In Mommsen and Ketteneker, *Fascist Challenge.*

Snell, J. *The Outbreak of the Second World War: Design or Blunder?* London: D. C. Heath, 1962.

Sobel, Robert. *The Impact of Public Opinion on Foreign Policy Since Vietnam: Constraining the Colossus.* Oxford: Oxford University Press, 1990.

Sorenson, Theodore C. *Kennedy.* New York: Harper and Row, 1965.

Squitieri, Tom. "General Says New War Could Strain Military." *USA Today,* February 17, 2005.

———. "Reserve, Guard Raise Recruiting Age." *USA Today,* March 22, 2005.

Stein, Janice Gross. "Deterrence and Compellance in the Gulf, 1990–91." *International Security* 17:2 (Fall 1992): 147–179.

Stewart, Graham. *Burying Caesar: The Churchill–Chamberlain Rivalry.* New York: Overlook Press, 1999.

Stillman, Edmund, and William Pfaff. *The Politics of Hysteria: The Sources of Twentieth-Century Conflict.* New York: Harper and Row, 1964.

Strategic Survey 2004/5: An Evaluation and Forecast of World Affairs. London: International Institute for Strategic Studies, 2005.

Stueck, William. *Rethinking the Korean War: A New Diplomatic and Strategic History*. Princeton: Princeton University Press, 2002.

Taylor, A. J. P. *The Origins of the Second World War*. London: Hamish Hamilton, 1961.

Taylor, Telford. *Munich: The Price of Peace*. Garden City, NY: Doubleday, 1979.

"Text of Truman's 'Report to the Nation' on the Korean War." *New York Times*, September 2, 1950.

Thomas, Martin. "France and the Czechoslovak Crisis." *Diplomacy and Statecraft* 10: 2–3 (July/November 1999): 122–159.

Thornton, Richard C. *Odd Man Out: Truman, Mao, and the Origins of the Korean War*. Washington, DC: Brassey's, Inc., 2000.

Tomes, Robert R. "Relearning Counterinsurgency Warfare." *Parameters* 34:1 (Spring 2004): 16–28.

Truman, Harry S. *Memoirs*. Vol. 2, *Years of Trial and Hope, 1946–1952*. Garden City, NY: Doubleday, 1955–56.

Vital, David. "Czechoslovakia and the Powers, September 1938." *Journal of Contemporary History* 1:4 (October 1966): 37–67.

Wark, Wesley K. *The Ultimate Enemy: British Intelligence and Nazi Germany, 1933–1939*. Ithaca, NY: Cornell University Press, 1985.

Watt, Donald Cameron. "British Intelligence and the Coming of the Second World War in Europe." In *Knowing One's Enemies: Intelligence Assessment Before the Two World Wars*. Edited by Ernest R. May. Princeton: Princeton University Press, 1984.

———. *How War Came: The Immediate Origins of the Second World War, 1938–1939*. New York: Pantheon Books, 1989.

Webster's New World Dictionary and Thesaurus. 2nd ed. New York: Hungry Minds, 2002.

Weinberg, Gerhard L. *Germany, Hitler, and World War II: Essays in Modern German and World History*. New York: Cambridge University Press, 1995.

———, ed. *Hitler's Second Book: The Unpublished Sequel to* Mein Kampf. Translated by Krista Smith. New York: Enigma Books, 2003.

———. "Reflections on Munich After 60 Years." *Diplomacy and Statecraft* 10:2–3 (July/November 1999): 1–12.

Weisman, Jonathan, and Renae Merle. "Pentagon Scales Back Arms Plan." *Washington Post*, January 5, 2005.

Wheeler-Bennett, J. W. *Munich: Prologue to Tragedy*. New York: Duell, Sloan and Pearce, 1948.

Young, Robert J. *France and the Origins of the Second World War*. New York: St. Martin's Press, 1996.

———. "French Military Intelligence and Nazi Germany, 1938–1939." In *Knowing One's Enemies: Intelligence Assessment Before the Two World Wars*. Edited by Ernest R. May. Princeton: Princeton University Press, 1984.

———. *In Command of France: French Foreign Policy and Military Planning 1933–1940*. Cambridge: Harvard University Press, 1978.

———. "The Use and Abuse of Fear: France and the Air Menace in the 1930s." *Intelligence and National Security* 2:4 (October 1987): 88–109.

Index

Abwehr, 41
Abyssinia, 50
Afghanistan, 6, 82, 108
  public opinion on, 101
aggressor states
  characteristics of, 6–7
    and appeasement, 22–23
  deterrence and, 120
  objectives of, 11
airpower
  Britain and, 37
  of Germany, 137n125
    misreading of, 51–55
  Roosevelt and, 61
Allison, Graham, 105
al Qaeda, 82, 115
  conflation with Iraq, 84
  destruction of
    feasibility of, 85–86
    as objective, 84
  motivations of, 87–88
Amery, Leo, 58
Anglo-French appeasement
  Chamberlain and, 23–24
  design of, 23
  failure of, causes of, 67–72
  lessons from, 73–110
  sources of, 13–66
Anglo-German Naval Agreement, x, 50

Anti-Comintern Pact, 59
appeasement
  Churchill on, v, 11
  conditions for, 22–23
  influence of, Herder on, 8–9
  nature of, 10–11
  term, 10–11, 112
  See also Anglo-French appeasement
asymmetrical warfare, 82, 100–101
  China and, 86–87
Australia, 37
Austria, 28, 48–49
aviation system, vulnerability of, 104

Bacevich, Andrew, 3
Baldwin, Stanley, 51
Beck, Ludwig, 41
Beck, Robert J., 66
Belgium, 8, 27–28
Bell, P. M. H., 8, 14, 17, 53, 63
Ben-Arie, Katriel, 46
Benes, Edward, 40, 136n106
Benjamin, Daniel, 85, 105
Bergen, Peter, 103
Bessarabia, 63
Biddle, Stephen, 86
Biddle, Tami Davis, 52
bin Laden, Osama, 88–89

bin Laden, Osama, 88–89
  versus Hitler, 115–16
  view of United States, 107–9
bombing, strategic, fear of, and appeasement, 51–52
Boot, Max, 81, 86
Bormann, Martin, 44
Britain
  Battle of, 52, 55
  dominions of, 36–37
  France's strategic dependence on, 38–47
  and Germany, 67–68
  and Hitler, 43
  military policy of, 34–35
  mobilization of troops, 36
  public opinion on war in, 56–57
  relations with United States, as appeasement, 11–12
  security situation in Thirties, 7–8, 65–66, 116
  and Soviet Union, 65, 70
  strategic overstretch of, 31–38, 90
  and Versailles Treaty, 20–21, 47, 49–50, 56–57
  World War I and, 14–15, 31–32
  See also under Anglo
Brzezinski, Zbigniew, 86–87, 89
Bullitt, William C., 50
Bush, George H. W., 4–5
Bush, George W., 3, 5, 80–81, 117–18
  and foreign policy, 83–84, 100
Bush Doctrine, 77

Cambon, Paul, 50
Canaris, Wilhelm, 41
Chamberlain, Neville, x, 8, 22, 66
  and appeasement, 23–24, 45
  and economic position, 31
  and Hitler, 15, 21–23, 44–45, 68
  and military policy, 35
  and public opinion, 58, 78
  and RAF, 35–36, 55
  and war, 42, 44
  and World War I, 14
chemical plants, vulnerability of, 104

China
  characteristics of, 6
  and irregular warfare, 86–87, 100–101
Churchill, Winston, xi
  and airpower, 53
  on appeasement, v, 11
  on Benes, 136n106
  on French army, 30
  on Munich Agreement, 40, 133n22
Clemenceau, Georges, 38
Clinton, William J., 5
Cohen, Eliot, 25
Cold War, versus Munich Agreement, 4
Cole, USS, 107
Committee of Imperial Defense, 32–33
Communism, fear of, and appeasement, 62–65
conscription
  Britain and, 35
  United States and, 60, 83
containment, 121
Cordesman, Anthony H., 83, 123
Council on Foreign Relations, 104
counterinsurgency
  in Iraq, 78–79
  training for, 88–89, 125
Craig, Gordon, 10
Crozier, Andrew, 23, 64
Cuban Missile Crisis, versus Munich Agreement, 4
Czechoslovakia, x, 1, 28
  Chamberlain and, 34
  importance of, 40–41
  Munich Agreement and, 41–43
  self-determination and, 21
  speculation on, 46

Daladier, Edouard, 22, 40, 43–45, 78
Defense Department, 82, 87–88
  and Iraq reconstruction, 122–24
  shortcomings of, 87–88
defense-offense balance
  Britain and, 32
  France and, 24–31
  importance of, 101–6

Defense Requirements Committee, 33–34
de Gaulle, Charles, 26
democratic governments, and public opinion, 77–78
deterrence
　and Hitler, 68–69
　nuclear, 120–22
　recommendations for, 89
Diamond, Larry, 124
domino theory, 4, 7
Duroselle, Jean-Baptiste, 28

Echevarria, Antulio, 83
economic issues
　Britain and, 31–33
　Versailles Treaty and, 48
Eisenhower, Dwight, 4
Environmental Protection Agency, 104
Estonia, 63
Europe
　current state of, 73
　after Nazi expansion, 19
　after World War I, 18

Federal Emergency Management Agency, 106
Fest, Joachim, 16
Finland, 63
Flynn, Stephen, 103
force, consistency in threats and use of, 106–9
foreign policy, and military force, 81–89
France
　and Anglo-German Naval Agreement, 50
　channel coast of, strategic value of, 37
　and German airpower, 54
　military inflexibility of, 24–31
　mobilization of troops, 36
　public opinion on war in, 57
　security situation in Thirties, 7–8, 46–47, 116
　and Soviet Union, 62, 64–65, 70
　strategic dependence on Britain, 38–47

and Versailles Treaty, 38
World War I and, 15, 25–26
See also Anglo-French appeasement
Fry, Michael Graham, 37
Furnia, Arthur H., 39

Gamelin, Maurice, 27–28
George, Alexander, 10
Gerges, Fawaz A., 88–89
Germany
　airpower of, 137n125
　　misreading of, 51–55
　deterrence of, 71–72
　expansion of, 19
　military leadership of
　　and Czechoslovakia, 41–42
　　and Hitler, 70
　　and war, 71–72
　mobilization of troops, 36, 40–41
　and Versailles Treaty, 47–51
　after World War I, 18
　See also Anglo-French appeasement; Nazi regime
Goering, Hermann, 42–43
Gooch, John, 25
Gray, Colin, 85, 120–21
Grenada, 4
guerrilla warfare, 82
Gulf War
　consistency in threats and use of force in, 106–7
　versus Munich Agreement, 4–5
　threat miscalculation in, 74

Haass, Richard, 81, 119
Hammes, Thomas X., 87–88
Harries, Owen, 109–10
Hearder, Harry, 8–9
Henlein, Konrad, 42
hindsight
　on Hitler's ambitions, 20
　nature of, 10–11, 117–18
Hitler, Adolf, 1
　on airpower, 51
　ambitions of, 68
　　Anglo-French failure

to grasp, 15–24
versus bin Laden, 115–16
and Chamberlain, 15, 21–23,
    44–45
and Czechoslovakia, 42–43
and foreign policy, 16
ideology of, 16–17, 20
as incomparable, 111–12
as unappeasable, 22, 67
as undeterrable, 68–72
view of Britain, 37–38
view of United States, 58
and war, 42, 44, 70
Ho Chi Minh, 7, 112
Holocaust
deterrence and, 72
and perspective on appease-
    ment, 10
homeland security, 102–6
assessment of, recommenda-
    tions for, 128
Hoover, Herbert, 50
Hussein, Saddam, 5, 7
conflation with al Qaeda, 84
versus Hitler, 71, 112
view of United States, 106–7

Inskip, Thomas, 52, 55
insurgency
characteristics of, 88
in Iraq, 78–79
intelligence community
failure of, 75–76
recommendations for, 76–77
International Institute for Strategic
    Studies, 88
Iran, 81, 89
Iraq
characteristics of, 7
reconstruction of, 84–85
state building in, 122–23
state disintegration in, 80
transformation of
    feasibility of, 85–86
    as objective, 84
See also Gulf War; Operation
    Iraqi Freedom
Islamic terrorism, characteristics of,
    115

Italy, 32–33, 69, 134n43

Japan, Britain and, 33, 37
Jervis, Robert, 7, 54
Johnson, Dominic, 54, 74
Johnson, Lyndon B., 4, 79

Kagan, Frederick W., 84
Kaplan, Robert, 86
Katrina, Hurricane, 106
Kearns, Doris, 4
Kennedy, John F., 4
Kennedy, Paul, 11, 22
Kershaw, Ian, 44
Keynes, John Maynard, 48
Khrushchev, Nikita, 6
Kiesling, Eugenia, 26
Kim Il-sung, 106
Kissinger, Henry, 27, 46–47, 49
Knopf, Jeffrey, 121
Korb, Lawrence, 81–82
Korean War
consistency in threats and use
    of force in, 106–7
versus Munich Agreement, 3–4
sustaining public support for, 78
threat miscalculation in, 74
Kosovo intervention, 6, 107
versus Munich Agreement, 5
Kristallnacht, 59
Kuwait, 4–5
See also Gulf War

Lammers, Donald N., 65
Latvia, 63
League of Nations, ix, 38, 62
Lebanon, 107
Lend Lease program, 62
Liddell Hart, B. H., 35
Lindberg, Charles A., 53
Lloyd George, David, 5151
Lonsdale, David J., 83
Ludlow Amendment, 138n150

MacDonald, C. A., 61
MacMillan, Margaret, 17
Maginot line, 24, 27, 81
Mao Zedong, 111–12
May, Ernest R., 69–70

McCaffrey, Barry, 82
McDonough, Frank, 14
Mediterranean, Britain and, 32
Mein Kampf (Hitler), 68
Merry, Robert, 101, 112
Metz, Steven, 88
Meyers, Richard B., 87
Middle East, transformation of, 118
   as objective, 84
military force
   foreign policy and, 81–89
   relation to politics, 122–24
Millen, Raymond, 88
Milosevich, Slobodan, 5
Monroe Doctrine, 11
Moskos, Charles, 83
Muller, Klaus-Jurgen, 41–42
Munich Agreement, x, 1, 40–46
   Churchill on, 40, 133n22
Munich analogy
   influence of, 1–12
   recommendations for, 112–13
Murray, Williamson, 14–15, 41
Mussolini, Benito, 28, 42, 50, 69
Myers, Richard, 81

National Security Council, 123–24
Nazi regime, 68
   as incomparable, 111–12
   nature of, Anglo-French failure
     to grasp, 15–24
   territorial expansion of, *19*
   See also Germany
neoconservatives, theory of history
   of, 3
Neutrality Act, 60
New Zealand, 37
Nicaragua, 4
Nixon, Richard, 4, 79
Non-Aggression Pact, x, 62–63
North Korea, 81, 89
North Vietnam, characteristics of,
   7
nuclear deterrence, 120–22
nuclear terrorism, vulnerability to,
   105

offense. *See* defense-offense balance
OOTW. *See* operations other than

war
Operation Iraqi Freedom
   casualties in, 79
   as detour, 84–85
   effects of, 87–89
   evaluation of, 117–18
   military mismatch in, 83
   versus Munich Agreement, 2–3,
     5
   strategic overextension in, 80–
     85
   threat miscalculation in, 74–75
   versus Vietnam War, 78–79
operations other than war (OOTW),
   82
   forces dedicated to, recommen-
     dations for, 87, 124–27
   resources required for, 83
   term, 140n15
Overy, Richard, 35, 43
Oxford Union, 56

Pakistan, 108
Pape, Robert, 84
Parker, R. A. C., 47
Pearl Harbor, xi, 75
Perle, Richard, 2, 71
Pétain, Philippe, 25–26
Pius XI, pope, 29
Poland, x, 8, 22, 41, 44, 63
politics, relation to military force,
   122–24
Potter, David, 10
Powell, Colin, 109
preemptive war, versus preventive
   war, 119
preventive war
   alternative to, 119–20
   versus deterrence, 89
   evaluation of, 118–22
   and Hitler, 70–71
   risks of, 101
public opinion
   analogy and, 1
   and appeasement, 55–58
   democratic governments and,
     77–81
   on war on terrorism, 101

Quadrennial Defense Review, 89
Quarantine Speech, 61

racial ideology, Hitler and, 16–17, 20, 68–69
RAF. *See* Royal Air Force
Rand Corporation, 88–89, 125
Reagan, Ronald, 4
regime change, and Hitler, 71
Rhineland, 28–29, 38
Rice, Condoleezza, 122
Rich, Norman, 16–17, 58, 68
Richardson, J. L., 69
Rock, Stephen, 7, 10, 22–24
rogue states. *See* aggressor states
Roosevelt, Franklin Delano, ix, 58–59, 61, 75
Rowse, A. L., 58
Royal Air Force (RAF), xi, 35–36, 51–52, 55
Rumsfeld, Donald, 2
Russia, and World War I, 49

Schacht, Hjalmar, 20, 44
Schmidt, Paul O., 44
self-determination, principle of, 21, 47, 66
Shirer, William, 29, 45
Simon, Steven, 85, 105
Smuts, Jan, 50
Somalia, 107
South Korea, 106
Soviet Union, 73
    characteristics of, 6
    and Czechoslovakia, 46
    distrust of, 70
        and appeasement, 62–65
Speer, Albert, 16
Stalin, Josef, 6, 63–64, 70, 106, 111
State Department, exclusion of, 123
strategic bombing, fear of, and appeasement, 51–52
strategic environment
    and military force, 82
    of Thirties versus today, 73–74, 113–15
strategic overextension
    Britain and, 31–38

dangers of, 89–101
struggle, term, 87
suicide attacks, 84
support for war
    mobilizing, 77–78
    sustaining, 78–81

Taiwan, 6, 86
Taliban, 6
Taylor, A. J. P., 15
ten-year rule, 32
terrorism, 82
    China and, 87
    Islamic, characteristics of, 115
    term, 87
    war on. *See* war on terrorism
terrorist organizations
    delegitimization of
        feasibility of, 86–89
        as objective, 84
    destruction of
        feasibility of, 86–89
        as objective, 84
    motivations of, 87–88
Thompson, Loren, 126
threat miscalculation
    of Germany's airpower, 51–55
    penalties of, 74–75
Trenchard, Hugh, 51
Truman, Harry S, 3–4, 118–19

United States
    and defense, 101–6
    foreign policy, 83–84, 100
        effects of, 109–10
        versus military force, 82–89
    isolationism of, 49, 138n150
        and appeasement, 58–62
    and League of Nations, 38
    lessons on appeasement, 73–110
    military force
        composition of, 81–82
        demands on, 80–81
        versus foreign policy objectives, 82–89
        prestige of, 109–10
        recommendations

for, 124–28
   recruiting, 82–83
and preventive war, 118–22
relations with Britain, 11–12
and strategic overextension, 89–
   101

Vansittart, Robert, 41
Versailles, Treaty of, ix, 7, 62
   Britain and, 20–21, 47, 49–50,
      56–57
   elements of, 47–49
   France and, 38
   geography of, *18*
   guilt over, 47–51
   Hitler and, 16–17, 20–22
Vietnam War
   influence of, 107–8
   versus Munich Agreement, 4
   versus Operation Iraqi Freedom,
      78–79
   sustaining public support for, 78
   threat miscalculation in, 74
Vuillemin, Joseph, 54

war, term, 87
war on terrorism
   defense-offense balance in, 102–
      6
   versus Iraq war, 84–85
   objectives of, 84–85
      feasibility of, 85–89
      realistic, 89–90
   term, 87
weapons of mass destruction
   (WMD), control of
   feasibility of, 89
   as objective, 84
Weinberg, Gerhard, 17, 45
Wheeler-Bennett, J. W., 44
Wiedemann, Fritz, 43
Wilson, Horace, 43
Wilson, Woodrow, 38, 62
WMD. *See* weapons of mass destruction
World War I
   and Britain, 31–32
   and France, 25–26
   geographical effects of, *18*

impact of, 13–15
and public opinion on war, 56–
   57
United States and, 58
See also Versailles, Treaty of
World War II
   buildup to, chronology of, ix–xi
   and perspective on appease-
      ment, 10

Young, Robert J., 10, 24, 39, 64–65

Zarqawi, Abu Musab, 88–89
Zawahri, Ayman, 108